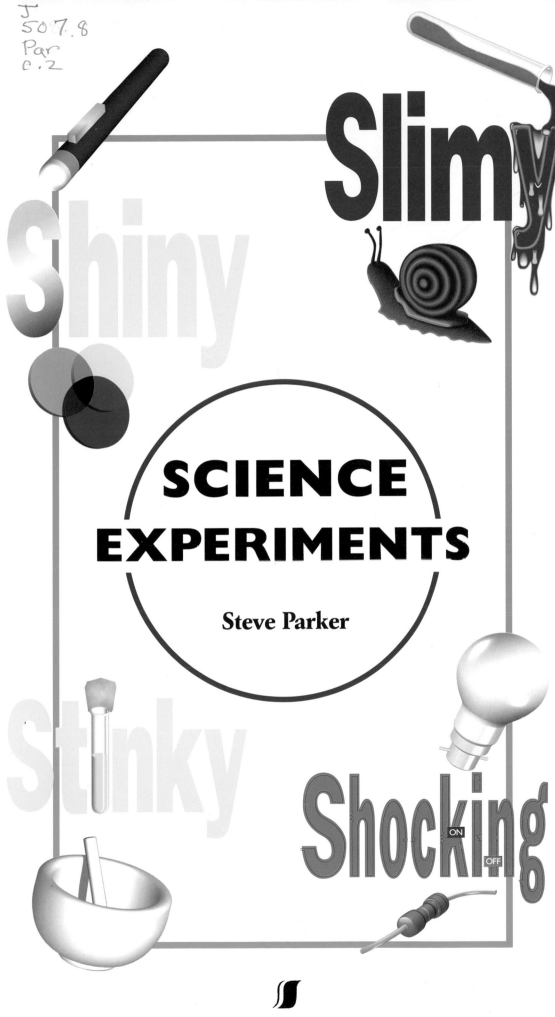

SCIENCE EXPERIMENTS

Steve Parker

Slimy

Shiny

Stinky

Shocking

Sterling Publishing Co., Inc.
New York

A QUARTO CHILDREN'S BOOK

Library of Congress Cataloging-in-Publication Data Available

1   3   5   7   9   10   8   6   4   2

First Paperback edition published in 2000 by
Sterling Publishing Co., Inc.
387 Park Avenue South, New York, N.Y. 10016

Copyright © 1998 Quarto Children's Books Ltd

Distributed in Canada by Sterling Publishing Co., Inc.
c/o Canadian Manda Group, One Atlantic Avenue, Suite 105
Toronto, Ontario, Canada M6K 3E7

This book was designed by Quarto Children's Books Ltd
The Fitzpatrick Building
188–194 York Way
LONDON N7 9QP

ART EDITOR Miranda Snow
EDITOR Diana Briscoe
ASSISTANT EDITOR Alice Bell
DESIGNER Keith Watson
PICTURE MANAGER Pernilla Nissen
PHOTOGRAPHY Laura Wickenden
ILLUSTRATION Patrick Mulrey & Stuart Simpson

PICTURE ACKNOWLEDGMENTS
Ace Photo Agency: page 4c
BT Corporate Pictures / ND Comtec: page 16tr
The Image Bank: page 22tr
Life File: page 26tr
Courtesy of NASA: page 11 bl
Ronald Grant Collection: pages 6tr, 12tr

Printed and bound in Singapore.

Sterling ISBN 0-8069-5914-2

Contents

Shiny Science   **5–22**

LIGHT IN THE DARKNESS
1   Transparent, translucent, opaque 6–7
2   Light, dark, and shadows   8
3   Shadows "in reverse"   9
4   Studying shadows   10–11

BOUNCING LIGHT
5   Reflected light   12
6   In the mirror   13
7   Lots of reflections   14
8   Make a periscope   15
9   Curved mirrors   15

BENDING LIGHT
10 Light and liquids   16
11 Magic mirror   17

LIGHT AND LENSES
12 What do lenses do?   18
13 See the point!   19
14 More about lenses   20

WAVES AND COLORS
15 Rainbow colors   21
16 Make a rainbow   22

Shocking Science   **23–37**

STATIC ELECTRICITY
17 Making static   24–25
18 What can you charge?   26–27
19 How charges leak away   28
20 More about static   29

CIRCUITS AND SWITCHES
21 Make a circuit   30
22 Switched-on circuits   31
23 Series and parallel   32

CONDUCTORS AND INSULATORS
24 The insulating board   33
25 Can it conduct?   34

ELECTRICITY AND MAGNETISM
26 Electrical magnetism   35
27 Make an electromagnet   36
28 Make a stronger electromagnet   37

Slimy Science   **38–64**

TESTING SIMPLE SLIMES   38
29 Choose your slimes!   41
30 How runny are slimes?   42–43
31 How sticky are slimes?   44–45
32 How stringy are slimes?   46
33 How creepy are slimes?   47

How Slimes Change
34 Do slimes dry out?   48
35 Slimes and cold   49
36 Slimes and warmth   49

Measuring Slimes
37 Making a slimometer   50–51
38 Comparing slimes   52
39 Pouring slimes   53
40 Checking up on slimes   54
41 Making powdered slime   54
42 Are watery slimes less slimy? 55
43 Dissolving slimes   56
44 Absorbing slimes   56–57
45 Filtering slimes   57
46 Colors of slimes   58
47 Slimes in pipes   59

Why are Some Plants Slimy?
48 Turn an egg into slime!   61
49 Plant slimes   62
50 Animal slimes   63–64

Stinky Science   65–91

The Sense of Smell
51 Sight, touch, and smell   67
52 Touch and smell   68
53 Less touch, more smell   68–69
54 Even less touch, more smell 69
55 Smell alone   70
56 Smell with your mouth!   70–71

Strengths of Smell
57 How faint can smells be? 72–73
58 Which smell is strongest?   73
59 Confusing smells   74
60 Battle of the smells   74–75
61 Why smells fade   75
62 Releasing smells   76–77
63 Smells that make you cry   77

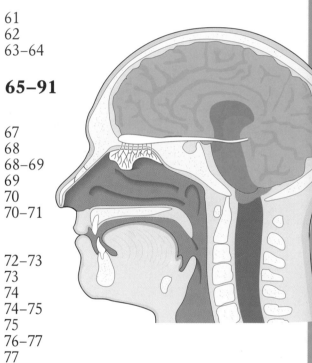

Nice 'n' Nasty Smells
64 Top of the smells   78–79
65 The next great chip   80
66 Not a rotten egg?   81
67 Memories are made of smells 82
68 Get-well smells   82–83

The Smell Industry
69 "Fresh" air?   84–85
70 Your favorite perfume   85
71 Make your own perfumes   86–87

Scratch 'n' Sniff
72 Smelly technology   88–89
73 Smelling blind!   90–91

Glossary of Terms   92–94

Index   95–96

INTRODUCING LIGHT

Without light, we'd all be in the dark. The Sun's natural light brightens up our world and lets us work, rest, and play. At night or in dark rooms, we flick a switch to turn on electric light bulbs and lamps. Our sense of sight depends on our eyes detecting light. We see to move around, stay safe, learn skills, enjoy ourselves, and communicate with others.

Light is also a useful energy source. Green plants catch the Sun's light energy to live and grow. In the future, solar power stations may do the same to produce electricity. The science of light—optics—has given us hundreds of gadgets that work with or by light, from eyeglasses, telescopes, and microscopes, to cameras, films, and television.

In this section you study light and how it works. You can find out about shadows, mirrors and reflections, lenses and prisms, and colors. Record your findings in a notebook.

- **Warning:** some light is so bright it can harm your eyes. Never look straight into a flashlight, light bulb or lamp, even if its beam is reflected in a mirror or passing through a lens. NEVER EVER look at the Sun.

LIGHT IN THE DARKNESS

Not much more than 100 years ago, there were no electric light bulbs. People used other types of lighting, such as gas lamps, candles, oil lamps, and fires. These flickered and were not very bright compared to today's modern light bulbs. However, they were good for making eerie, wobbly shadows on the wall. Shadows show one of light's basic features— its rays usually travel in straight lines.

Experiment 1
Transparent, translucent, opaque

You can see through most windows, unless, of course, the glass is "frosted." Frosted glass lets some light through, but doesn't provide a clear view. Curtains prevent us from seeing anything through a window. Glass is transparent, frosted glass is translucent, and curtains are opaque.

1 Gather a selection of materials such as a newspaper, a clear plastic bag (such as a freezer storage bag), a thin cotton T-shirt, some crêpe paper, tracing paper, and so on. You also need a penlight and clear but colored plastic, like candy wrappers.

2 Hold one of the items in front of your face, about 12 in. (30 cm) away. Shine the penlight through it from about 4 in. (10 cm) on the other side. DO NOT point the penlight beam directly into your eyes. Point it slightly sideways.

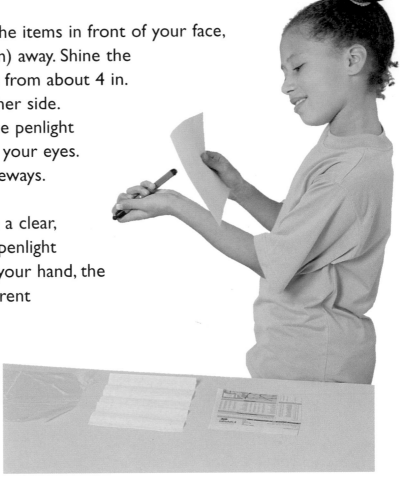

3 If you can see a clear, sharp view of the penlight and its beam, and your hand, the material is transparent (see-through). This is the case even if the view is colored or tinted.

4 If you can see the penlight's beam, but the view is unclear, blurred, hazy, or frosty, then the substance is translucent.

5 If you can't see anything, it's opaque! Try all the materials you have collected. Which is most transparent?

Experiment 2
Light, dark, and shadows

Lots of light is bright. Less light is dim, dull, or gloomy. No light is very dark, maybe even black. A shadow is an area of darkness with light around it.

1 You need a penlight, some black card, safety scissors, cotton thread or string, and a room with plain white or pale walls that you can make dark.

2 Shine the penlight at your hand from about 12 in. (30 cm) away. See how your hand is lit by the light.

3 See how the rest of the light goes past your hand and shines on the wall another 12 in. (30 cm) or so away. Light rays travel in straight lines. Your hand blocks some of them, leaving a dark patch on the wall—a shadow.

4 Cut out scary shapes, such as a spider, bat, and witch, from black card. Hang them on lengths of thread or string. Shine the penlight on them so they throw dark shapes on the wall. It's a Shadow Ghost Show!

5 Make the same shapes from a translucent material such as tracing paper. Are the shadows slightly less dark? Try using colored candy wrappers and see if you can make colored shadows.

German astronomer Johannes Kepler (1571–1630) studied how light goes in straight lines and casts shadows. He went on to figure out the exact paths or orbits of the planets around the Sun, called Kepler's laws of planetary motion. Kepler showed that planets do not go in circles. They travel in orbits which are ovals or ellipses.

Experiment 3
Shadows "in reverse"

One type of shadow is a dark area surrounded by light. But you can also have a light area surrounded by darkness—a shadow in reverse.

1 You need the equipment as for EXPERIMENT 2, plus a large sheet of stiff black card. Carefully cut a scary shape, such as a bat, out of the center of the card to make a hole.

2 Shine a penlight from about 12 in. (30 cm) away, through the hole in the card, onto a wall another 12 in. (30 cm) away.

3 The hole lets the light through, while the card blocks it. Now you have a light bat in a dark area instead of a dark bat in a light area.

4 Cut a much larger hole in the shape of a castle with several towers. This can be a background for the scary shapes from EXPERIMENT 2.

Experiment 4
Studying shadows

Shadows change size, depending on the distances between the light source and the object, and between the object and the wall or other surface.

1 Use a scary shape from EXPERIMENT 2, plus two rulers, Scotch tape, penlight, and tape measure. Tape the two rulers together lengthwise in an upside-down V shape. Tape or clip the shape near one end, as shown.

2 Clip the penlight to the end of the rulers, near the scary shape. It should shine past the shape onto a white wall or card about 18 in. (45 cm) away.

3 Measure the distance between the penlight and the shape. Also measure the total width of the shadow. Record the results in your notebook.

4 Move the shape along the rulers, farther from the penlight. Again, measure the distance from the penlight to the shape, and the width of the shadow. Do this several times. Is there any connection between the size of the shadow and the distance between the penlight and shape?

5 As you do this experiment, study the details of the shadow. How sharp are its edges? When is it clearest or most blurred?

SHADOWS

A shadow is created when rays of light are blocked by an opaque object in their path. The light rays travel in straight lines and cannot bend around the object. The result is a shadow. The smaller and more concentrated the light source, the sharper the shadow it produces.

The Sun itself is a very concentrated light source. It seems almost a point to us because it is so far away. One of the most dramatic types of shadow is a solar eclipse. The Moon travels between the Sun and the Earth, casting its shadow on the Earth's surface. Another dramatic shadow is produced during a lunar eclipse, when the Earth passes between the Sun and the Moon. When this occurs, a shadow of the Earth can then be seen moving slowly across the face of the Moon.

A view of a solar eclipse taken from the Apollo 12 spacecraft during its journey home from the Moon. The view was created when the Earth moved directly between the Sun and the Apollo 12 spacecraft.

BOUNCING LIGHT

In medieval times, people believed that light shone from their eyes onto their surroundings, so they could see. In fact, it's the other way around. Light comes from objects into our eyes. Some objects are light sources. That means they make their own light. The Sun, flames, and light bulbs are examples of this.

Most objects don't produce their own light. Light rays come from a light source such as the Sun, bounce off the object, and go into our eyes. Bouncing light is called *reflection*.

Experiment 5
Reflected light

Most things can be seen because they bounce light from something—the Sun or a lit light bulb—into the eyes.

1 Find materials such as aluminum foil, a glossy magazine, a bowl of water, a shiny plastic bag, a mirror and some black card.

2 Look at them in bright conditions. Some objects reflect most of the light and don't absorb the rays—a glossy magazine cover, for example. Others, such as black card, absorb all the light.

3 You see objects because light rays go toward them and bounce off into your eyes. While some reflect the light, they do not always give a reflection. The objects which give the best reflection are flat and "shiny" like a mirror. A mirror reflects nearly all the light that falls on it straight back again.

Experiment 6
In the mirror

This experiment shows how a mirror reflects or bounces light. It uses a slit-beam, a thin beam of almost parallel light rays.

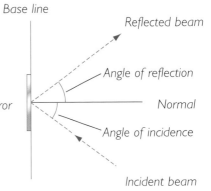

1 You need a penlight, mirror, some black and white card, pen, protractor, ruler, and safety scissors. Carefully cut a rectangle of black card measuring 4–6 in. (10–15 cm) and cut an upright slit about 2 in. (5 cm) long and 1/16 in. (4 mm) wide in the card's lower edge.

2 Draw a baseline near one edge of the white card. Draw another line at a right angle (90°) to it, to make a T shape (use the diagram to help you). This line is called the normal. Prop the mirror upright on the baseline, with the normal at its middle.

Base line

Reflected beam

Angle of reflection

Mirror

Normal

Angle of incidence

Incident beam

3 In dim conditions, shine a penlight through the slit in the card from about 6 in. (15 cm) away onto the mirror another 6 in. (15 cm) away. This gives a slit-beam. Aim the penlight down slightly to see the beam on the white card. Aim it at the junction of the T lines.

4 The slit-beam reflects off the mirror. Draw the path of the beam with a pen. The beam that points toward the mirror is called the incident beam. As it comes away, it is the reflected beam.

5 Measure the angles between the incident beam and the normal, and reflected beam and the normal. Are they about the same?

6 Repeat the experiment with the incident beam at a different angle. The angles of incidence and reflection should be the same. This shows a basic law of optics, the law of reflection.

Alhazen (965–1038) was an Egyptian scientist who studied mirrors, lenses, colors, and other topics related to light. He worked out the laws of reflection, and he threw out the old idea that light shone out from the eyes, saying instead that it shone in.

Experiment 7
Lots of reflections

In a mirror, the view or mirror-image is back to front—the other way around from real life. You can see this clearly with reflected writing! In this experiment we look at the reflection of a reflection.

1 You need two rulers taped in a V (see EXPERIMENT 4) plus two small mirrors. Tape or clip one at each end of the rulers.

2 Adjust a mirror to show your reflection. Wink your left eye. Which eye winks back?

3 Now angle the two mirrors so you look at one, and see the other reflected in it. You must see your face in the second mirror, so you may need to adjust the mirrors.

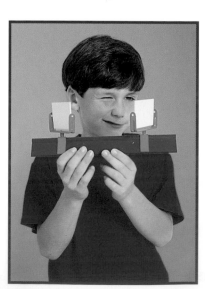

4 Now you see a reflection of a reflection. Does your face look the same as a normal mirror-image? Wink your left eye again. Which eye winks in the reflection this time?

Experiment 8
Make a periscope

Periscopes are useful for looking over, under, or around things. Submarine captains use them to see what's happening on the ocean's surface, while the submarine stays under the waves. All you need are two mirrors.

1 Use the same equipment as for EXPERIMENTS 4 and 7. Hold the V-shaped rulers upright. Fix or tape the lower mirror at about 45° toward you.

2 Do the same with the upper mirror, but angle it away from you. Then look into the lower mirror. Adjust it so you can see the upper mirror reflected in it. This is the principle of the periscope. Look at what the upper mirror reflects. Is the view back-to-front or upside down?

Experiment 9
Curved mirrors

Not all mirrors are flat. Look at make-up and shaving mirrors, and a car's rear-view mirror. Some are curved. This makes the reflection look either bigger (magnified) or smaller (diminished), depending on which way the mirror curves.

1 Find a smooth, shiny, curved object such as a spoon. Look at your reflection in the convex (bulging) surface. Is it the right way up, upside-down or distorted in any way? You probably look small and far away. Do the same into the concave (dished) surface. Does the view change? Are you big, small, the right way up, or upside down?

2 These changes are due to the way the curved mirror surface reflects the light rays. You can trace the path of the rays from your face to the mirror, and then up to your eyes.

Experiment 10
Light and liquids

Refraction or bending of light happens in transparent solids and transparent liquids. The amount of bending depends on the density of the liquid.

1 You need the same equipment as in EXPERIMENT 6, plus a square see-through glass or plastic container with flat sides, and a selection of see-through liquids such as water and clear cooking oil. (If you use cooking oil, be careful not to get it on your fingers or on the equipment.)

2 Follow EXPERIMENT 6, but instead of a mirror, use the container filled with water. Shine the light beam through it, swivel or twist it so it refracts the beam, and draw the beam, lines, and angles in front and behind.

3 Exchange the water for cooking oil. Repeat the experiment, putting the container in the same place, and shining the beam at the same angle. Is the angle, called the angle of refraction, different?

Refracted beam
Angle of refraction
Normal
Angle of incidence
Liquid
Incident beam
Container
Penlight
Slit card

4 Cooking oil is lighter or less dense than water. Its refractive index is therefore lower. Can you think of any other liquids to test?

Experiment 11
Magic mirror

Reflection turns to refraction at a certain angle—the critical angle. This creates some mysterious effects.

1 You need a mirror plus a deep bowl which is pale, opaque (not see-through), and filled with water. Hold the mirror in the water, about 3 in. (7.5 cm) under the surface on the far side of the bowl.

2 Angle the mirror so you can see yourself in it. Now place a finger into the water, just in front of the mirror, so that you can see see that, too. Light rays come from your face, refract at the water's surface, reflect off the mirror, refract again as they leave the water, and shine into your eyes.

3 Twist the mirror gradually, keeping your head and eyes steady. The view in the mirror, of the scene above the water's surface,

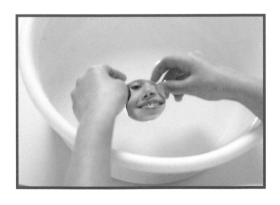

swings around, until suddenly you no longer see it. You now see a mirror-like surface with your finger sticking out. You've reached the critical angle, where refraction becomes reflection. The underside of the water's surface acts like a mirror.

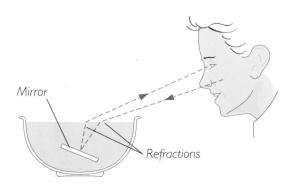

Mirror

Refractions

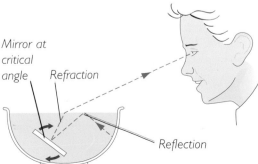

Mirror at critical angle   Refraction

Reflection

LIGHT AND LENSES

A lens is a curved shape of a transparent substance, like clear plastic or glass. It works by refracting light. *Convex lenses* bulge, or are thicker in the middle than around the edge. *Concave lenses* are like dishes, or thinner in the middle than around the edge. Lenses are vital parts in hundreds of machines, gadgets, and inventions. And in our own eyes they are essential!

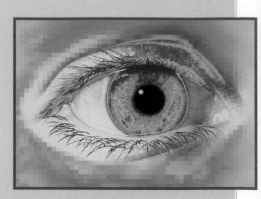

Experiment 12
What do lenses do?

A convex lens bends or refracts light beams so that they converge, or come together. This has the effect of making things look bigger, or magnified, when we see them through the lens.

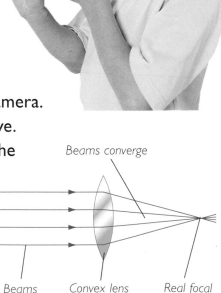

1 You need a large convex lens, from a science store or equipment like an old camera. Hold it about 10 in. (25 cm) from your eye. Put your fingertip about 2 in. (5 cm) on the other side.

2 See how the lens works as a magnifier. You may have to move it back and forth to get the best result.

Beams converge

Beams of light *Convex lens* *Real focal point*

3 A concave lens bends or refracts light beams so that they diverge, or spread apart. This has the effect of making things look smaller, or diminished, when they are seen through the lens. Try this with a concave lens from a science store or old equipment.

Experiment 13
See the point!

When a convex lens converges light rays, all the rays come together at one place, which is called the focal point (focus). The distance from the center of the lens to the focus is called the focal length. Lenses of different focal lengths are used for different jobs.

1 You need a convex lens (see EXPERIMENT 12), the V-shaped rulers (see EXPERIMENT 4), penlight, black card, white card, ruler, Scotch tape, safety scissors and dim surroundings. Cut a 4–6 in. (10–15 cm) rectangle of black card.

2 In the middle cut a cross shape of two slits, each about 2 in. (5 cm) long and $1/16$ in. (2 mm) wide.

3 Cut a V shape in the bottom long edge of the card so it fits on the rulers. Tape the card to the rulers as shown.

4 Tape or clip the penlight and card to the rulers as shown. This is your slit-beam device. It is similar to the one in EXPERIMENT 6, but now the beam it shines is cross-shaped.

5 Tape or clip a convex lens to the other end of the rulers, so the slit-beam cross shines through it. Hold a large piece of white card upright about 4 in. (10 cm) from the lens. See how the lens refracts (bends) the cross-beam and shines an image of it on the card.

6 Gradually move the card farther away from the lens. As you do this, the cross will shrink to a dot. The dot is the focal point of the lens, where all the light rays converge. The distance from the lens to the card is the focal length of the lens.

Dutch merchant Anton van Leeuwenhoek (1632–1723) traded textiles and cloths, but his hobby was using powerful pea-sized convex lenses as strong magnifiers, or microscopes. As a result of his hobby, he was one of the first people ever to see the tiny cells in blood, and microbes, such as bacteria and amoeba.

Experiment 14
More about lenses

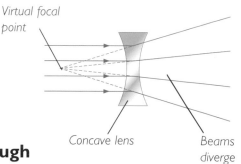

Virtual focal point

Concave lens

Beams diverge

The concave lens diverges or spreads light rays apart, which means they cannot all pass through one place behind the lens, the focal point. The rays look as if they come from right in front of the lens, called the virtual focal point.

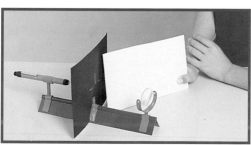

I Set up the equipment as in EXPERIMENT 13, but use a concave lens (see EXPERIMENT 12). Angle it slightly to the side, as shown.

2 Some light rays are refracted through the lens, but some reflect off the lens's glass surface, which works like a half-mirror. Position the card to catch them. They form a cross of light on the same side of the lens as the penlight.

3 Move the card back and forth until the cross-beam shrinks to a dot. This is the virtual focal point. The distance from lens to card is the focal length of the concave lens.

Italian scientist Galileo Galilei (1564–1642) used the newly invented telescope to study the night sky. He saw mountains on the Moon, and four moons around the planet Jupiter. His work led to great arguments in science and religion, about whether the Sun went around the Earth, or the Earth around the Sun.

Experiment 15
Rainbow colors

Color is a very important feature of light. A black-and-white world would be very boring! The color of an object depends on the color of the light waves it reflects into our eyes (see EXPERIMENT 16). How many different colors are there? Most people could probably distinguish more than a million, if they had time!

1 You need some liquid detergent, water, a cup or jar, and a small loop of thin wire or a bubble-blowing kit from a toy store.

2 Mix equal amounts of the detergent and water in the cup. Dip in the loop, take it out, and blow some bubbles!

3 Catch a bubble on the wire loop. Look at it carefully from different angles in strong light.

4 See how the bubble shows swirls of colored patterns, like rainbows. How many colors can you count before it pops?

Experiment 16
Make a rainbow

The idea that light travels as waves explains colors. The wavelength of a wave is the distance from the top or peak of one wave to the peak of the next. Different colors of light have different wavelengths. Red light has the longest. Green is in the middle. Blue and violet have the shortest wavelengths.

1 You need the V-shaped rulers and slit-beam as used in EXPERIMENT 13. Use just one upright slit, not a cross shape. You also need a triangular glass or plastic block, a prism, available from a science store or in old equipment like a camera.

2 Shine the slit-beam at the prism from about 4 in. (10 cm) away. Place a sheet of white card about 6 in. (15 cm) on the other side of the prism.

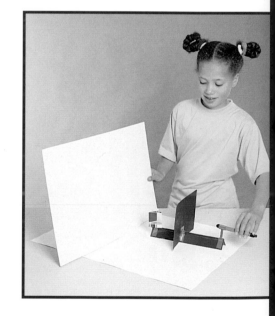

3 Turn the prism until it refracts the white slit-beam onto the card behind. The beam is now no longer pure white light. It's tinged with colors—a rainbow!

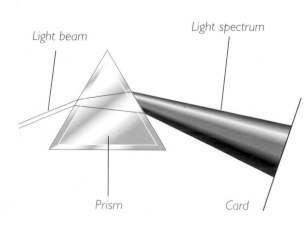

Light beam

Light spectrum

Prism

Card

4 The penlight's white light is a mixture of colored light waves of different wavelengths. The prism refracts each color by a slightly different amount— red least, and violet most. This rainbow-like range of colors is called the spectrum of light.

INTRODUCING ELECTRICITY

When there's a power cut, especially on a winter's night, you realize how much we depend on electricity. The lights and the heating go off. The TV, radio, and music system don't work. Without electricity, life would be very different.

We know that electricity is made in power stations and flows along wires to our homes, schools, factories, and offices. It's the most common and useful form of energy, powering hundreds of machines and devices—refrigerators, vacuum cleaners, washing machines, VCRs, fax machines, hair dryers, and computers.

Yet electricity is puzzling. You can't see or hear it. You can only see and hear its effects, like the light bulb's glow and the music from a CD player. And if it's used wrongly, high-voltage electricity from the wall socket can be very dangerous.

REMEMBER NEVER PLAY WITH THE PLUGS

STATIC ELECTRICITY

Electricity is based on the tiny particles called *atoms*, which make up everything in the Universe. Each atom has two parts. The nucleus in the middle is positive, and the electrons whizzing around it are negative.

Normally, the positive nucleus balances the negative electrons. But if electrons get separated from their nucleus, the balance is upset. The lonely electrons have negative charge, and the nucleus is positive.

Electricity is made by separating electrons from their nuclei. Scientists call it "separating charge." The negative charges may hang around and perhaps move in a short, sudden burst. This is *static electricity*.

Experiment 17
Making static

You can make an electric charge, or static electricity, simply by rubbing. The physical action or friction rubs billions of electrons away from their nuclei.

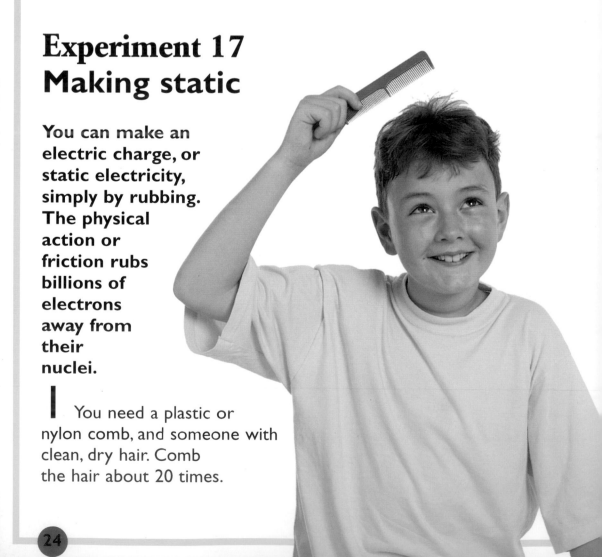

1 You need a plastic or nylon comb, and someone with clean, dry hair. Comb the hair about 20 times.

2 As hairs rub past the teeth of the comb, they both get charged with static electricity. Hold them near each other and the static charge attracts the strands. It's "flyaway hair!"

3 The charged comb may also attract and pick up very light objects, like small pieces of tissue paper. This attraction is a feature of static electricity. But gradually the charge fades and leaks away into the air.

Remember

Experiments with static electricity work best in dry conditions, when the weather and air are dry, too. Damp, humid air lets the charge leak away more quickly, so the experiments may not work so well.

Each atom has a central nucleus, which is positive, and negative electrons whizzing around it.

4 Now try making an electric charge by rubbing a balloon against your hair. The results may be even more spectacular!

Experiment 18
What can you charge?

Experiment with making static electricity by rubbing various substances, then seeing if they attract small, light objects such as pieces of tissue paper. This is called electrostatic attraction. The object you rub, and what you rub it with, are both important.

I You need a variety of objects made of nylon, plastic, or similar plastic-type materials—comb, spoon, pen, ruler, balloon, and soft-drink bottle. Also choose wooden or card items like a spoon, pencil, picture frame, and book cover. Add a selection of metal objects such

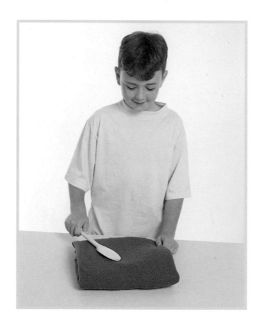

as a fork, ballpoint pen, round-ended scissors, and file, and you're ready to go.

2 Gather materials to do the rubbing, like a cotton T-shirt, wool sweater, garment made from artificial fibers such as acrylic or nylon, piece of fake fur, linen dishtowel, paper towel, and aluminum foil.

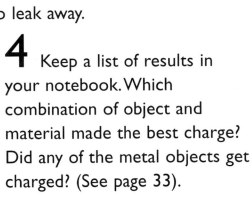

3 In a scientific way, rub each object with each material in turn, then see if it attracts the tiny pieces of tissue paper. This shows if it's charged with static. Allow a few minutes between each test, for any charge to leak away.

4 Keep a list of results in your notebook. Which combination of object and material made the best charge? Did any of the metal objects get charged? (See page 33).

Remember

Dust collects on a TV screen due to static electricity. The picture on the screen makes the screen charge up slightly. This attracts small, light particles—dust.

One of the first scientists to study electricity was Thales in ancient Greece. More than 2,500 years ago, he rubbed pieces of amber (gold-yellow sap from plants that has turned into solid, fossilized lumps). The rubbed amber attracted light objects like feathers. Our word "electricity" comes from elektron, Greek for amber.

Experiment 19
How charges leak away

When you rub an object to charge it with static, you produce billions of tiny charges, spread out evenly on its surface. But gradually these fade away or leak into damp air. They can also pass to another object that touches the charged object. This is called electrical conduction (see page 30).

1 You need a balloon and a large bowl of water. Rub the balloon on a wool sweater or something similar, to produce an electrostatic charge over its surface. Give it approximately 20 rubs.

2 The charged balloon is so light, it should stick to a wall by electrostatic attraction.

3 Repeat the experiment, but after rubbing, quickly push the balloon under the water. Shake it dry. Now will it stick to the wall? Probably not. The charge has leaked away into the water. Water is a conductor of electricity.

Experiment 20
More about static

Sometimes, static electricity doesn't attract or pull. It repels or pushes. This shows that there are two kinds of charges, positive and negative. A positively charged object attracts a negatively charged or a noncharged one. But it repels a positively charged object.

1 You need two balloons and some thin thread. Rub the balloons on some fabric to give them an electrostatic charge. See how each balloon by itself attracts small, light objects like pieces of tissue paper.

2 Tie a piece of thin thread to each balloon. Rub the balloons again to charge them, then hang them near each other. They should push each other away. They both have the same charge, so they repel each other.

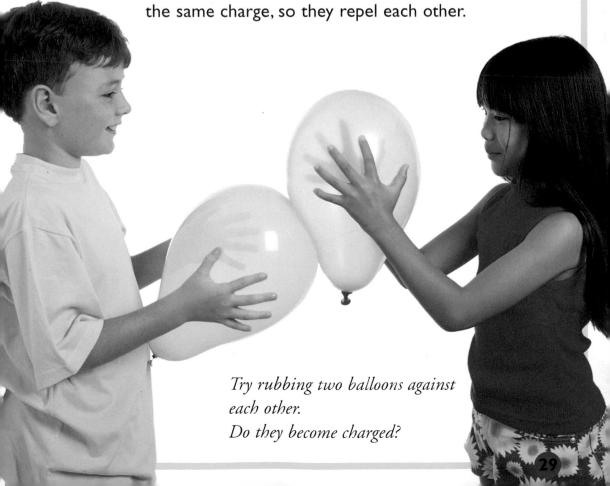

Try rubbing two balloons against each other.
Do they become charged?

CIRCUITS AND SWITCHES

The electricity that comes out of a battery is not static. It is moving—an *electric current*. It is the same type of charge as static electricity, involving electrons. But these electrons move along steadily.

Look closely at a battery. It has two connections or terminals, positive (+), and negative (−). Imagine the electric current flowing from the positive terminal to the negative one. But it must flow along something—a pathway of wires and similar parts, called *conductors*, between + and −. This circular path is called a *circuit*. A device in the circuit that can open a gap in it, or close this gap, is a *switch*.

Experiment 21
Make a circuit

In the simplest circuit, electricity flows from the battery along a wire, through an electric device such as a bulb, and along another wire, back to the battery.

1 You need one penlight battery, two insulated (plastic-coated) wires, a penlight bulb—and several pairs of hands! Hold the end of one wire against one battery terminal.

2 Hold this wire's other end against one connection of the bulb (its silver base). Hold one end of the second piece of wire against the bulb's other connection (its screw side).

3 Touch the free end of the wire to the other battery terminal. Electricity flows around the circuit—and makes the bulb glow.

Experiment 22
Switched-on circuits

You can make a circuit by connecting wires, and then break the circuit by disconnecting them. But an easier way is to use a switch. When closed or ON, it lets electricity flow.

1 You need insulated wires, penlight bulb in a bulb-holder, penlight battery, and an ON–OFF switch. Collect these separately or use parts from an educational kit, as shown.

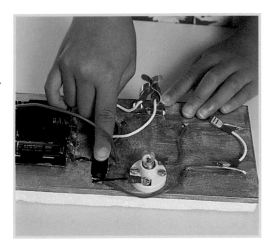

2 Make a circuit of the bulb, battery, switch, and wires. Turning the switch OFF makes a break in the circuit, and the bulb goes out.

BEWARE!

You should never try any of these experiments with anything except the equipment described here. Electricity can kill and you should always treat it with respect.

BRIGHT SPARKS OF HISTORY

A battery produces flowing electricity by a continuously separating charge, using combinations of chemicals inside it. But this only happens when the battery is connected into a circuit. The first battery, called an electric cell, was made by Italian scientist Alessandro Volta in 1800. Its steady flow of electric current led to all kinds of new experiments and electrical inventions.

Experiment 23
Series and parallel

Connecting batteries one after the other, end to end, is "in series." There's another way to connect them, side by side or "in parallel."

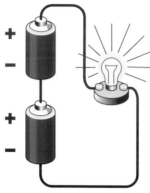

In series

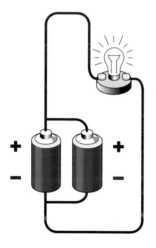

In parallel

1 Use insulated wires, a 3-volt penlight bulb in its holder, and two 1.5-volt penlight batteries, as shown in the diagrams. Or adapt an educational-type science kit, as shown in the photographs.

2 Connect the batteries one after the other, in series (diagram upper left). Their strengths or voltages add up—
1.5 + 1.5 = 3 volts
and the bulb glows brightly.

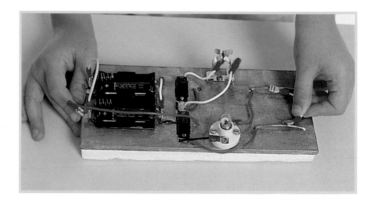

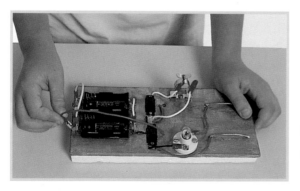

3 Now connect the batteries side by side, in parallel (diagram middle left). Like this the voltages of bulb and batteries do not add up, so the bulb glows less brightly. But it will glow for longer!

Remember When linking batteries in series, always join the + of one to the − of the next. In parallel, always join the + of one to the + of the other. Otherwise, you can damage the batteries.

CONDUCTORS AND INSULATORS

Electricity cannot move through everything. Otherwise, it would leak out of a battery into the air all the time! Electricity only flows through certain materials and substances—*conductors*. Electricity does not pass through other substances—*insulators*.

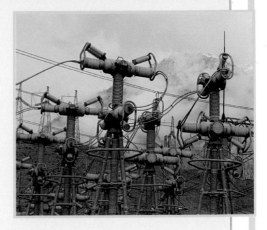

Experiment 24
The insulating board

Electrical circuits use conductors made of wire, on a board made of a special insulating material.

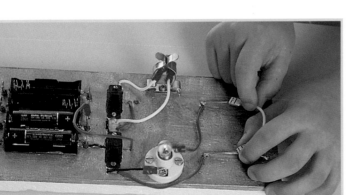

I Look at some electrical circuits, such as an educational-type science kit or a circuit board from an old electrical gadget. (Make sure it is NOT connected to the electrical supply!)

2 See that the board is made of a special material, like plastic. This is a good insulator.

3 Make a circuit as described in EXPERIMENT 21. Include part of the board in the circuit. Does the bulb glow? No!

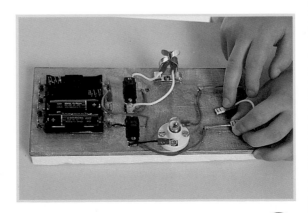

Experiment 25
Can it conduct?

Try common items to see if they are conductors and carry electricity, or if they are insulators and prevent it from passing along a circuit.

1 Make a circuit with a penlight bulb, battery, and insulated wires (see EXPERIMENT 21), or adapt an educational-type science kit. But leave a gap in the circuit.

2 Bridge the gap by touching various household items to the ends of the wires. If they are good conductors, the bulb shines brightly. If they are good insulators, it stays off.

3 Try things made of wood, metal, plastic, wool, rubber, leather, paper, and card. Record the results in your notebook. Do the conductors have anything in common?

ELECTRICITY AND MAGNETISM

For hundreds of years, people confused static electricity and *magnetism*, because both have the power to attract or repel. Now we know that electricity and magnetism are not the same. But they are not different, either! One can be turned into the other. In fact, the links between these two basic forces have given us the electromagnet, electric motor, and many other devices.

Experiment 26
Electrical magnetism

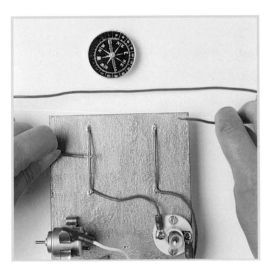

As electricity flows through a conductor, it makes an invisible magnetic force or magnetic field around the wire.

1 You need a small compass and an insulated wire carrying about 9–12 volts of electricity. Use a small 9-volt battery, or a battery case containing four small 3-volt batteries, as in some portable electrical devices. Or adapt an educational-type science kit, as shown. (DO NOT USE A VEHICLE BATTERY!)

2 Connect the battery terminals directly to the wire's two ends, with a straight part near the compass. This makes a direct path for electricity along the wire—a short circuit. It drains the battery fast, so do the experiment quickly!

3 Briefly touch the wires to make the circuit. Electricity flows and sets up a magnetic field near the wire. This affects the compass needle, and it flicks around.

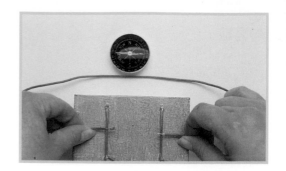

Experiment 27
Make an electromagnet

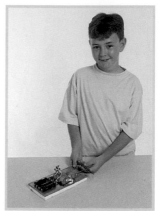

The magnetic field around a wire is quite weak. Make it stronger and more concentrated by winding the wire into a coil, with an iron rod in the middle. You've made an electromagnet!

1 Use similar equipment as in EXPERIMENT 26. Wind a very long piece of insulated wire around an iron nail. Touch the ends of the wire to the battery terminals.

2 Electricity flows through the wire and makes a magnetic field, turning the rod into an electromagnet. How many metal paper clips can it lift?

3 Disconnect the wire. The magnetism disappears, and the paper clips fall off. An electromagnet differs from the usual permanent magnet because you can turn it on and off.

Remember
A circuit with only batteries and wires allows lots of electricity (electric current) to flow very fast. The batteries will soon wear out or discharge. Do this experiment in short bursts of 2-3 seconds.

Experiment 28
Make a stronger electromagnet

The more turns of wire in the coil of an electromagnet, the stronger its magnetism. And the higher the voltage, the stronger it is, too.

1 Make the electromagnet as in EXPERIMENT 27. But use an even longer length of insulated wire, winding a second coil on top of the first.

2 Try more volts, too, using four batteries as in EXPERIMENT 26. How many paper clips can the magnet lift now?

Neon light

Las Vegas is well known for its bright neon lights, but what is neon light? A glass tube is filled with gas and an electric current is passed through it. The gas used affects the color of the light produced. Neon, for example, always gives off a red light.

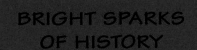

BRIGHT SPARKS OF HISTORY

Two rival scientists made many advances in electricity—Joseph Henry (1797–1878) and Michael Faraday (1791–1867). In the United States, Henry improved electromagnet design and worked on turning magnetism into electricity. In England, Faraday did similar studies and devised early types of electric motor, transformer, and generator.

TESTING SIMPLE SLIMES

How many slimy things have you touched today? For example, have you blown your nose?! For the following experiments, you need to collect a variety of slimy, sticky, and gooey substances which are safe to handle and fun to test. Here are lots of ideas to get you started. Some of them are dry powders, grains, or granules, but they become slimy or sticky when you add water or another liquid.

Bathroom
Hair shampoo
  and conditioner
Hand lotion
Shaving cream
Moisturizing cream
Sunscreen and
  sunblock oils
Vapor-rubs for
  blocked noses
Safe skin ointment
Deodorants and
  anti-perspirants
Toothpaste

Kitchen
Butter, margarine,
  and similar
  spreads
Cooking oils and
  fats
Peanut butter
Eggs
Shortening
Flour and corn
  starch
Soup powders,
  instant soups
Liquid detergent
Sauce and ketchup
Yogurt
Mayonnaise
Jell-o
Milk shakes
Whipped desserts
Molasses and syrup
Honey and
  preserves
Thick juices
Tomato paste
Creamy cheese
Squishy foods like
  avocado

Crafts and hobbies
Artist paint like oil
  paint and acrylics
Joke slimes from
  the toy store
Crazy-foam, squirty-
  string, and similar
  party substances
Wallpaper paste
Lubricating oil
Lubricating grease
Safe glue

Warning
Some slimy substances are dangerous. They can affect your skin, eyes, nose, and breathing, and they might make you very ill.
- Always read and follow the instructions on the containers.
- Look for hazard signs and symbols.
- Beware of slimes from the cleaning cupboard, garage, and basement.
- Never mess with unfamiliar slimes.
- Always cover surfaces with newspaper before doing your experiments—some slimes may stain if spilled.

INTRODUCING SLIMES

Every day we encounter slimes. Some are obviously slimy, like a slow slug sliding along a path, or the clear, slippery "white" from a not-quite-cooked, soft-boiled egg. Certain people don't like to touch them, and may even shudder at the thought. Yet other slimy substances seem more friendly, and we don't mind touching them at all. In fact, we even smear them on our bodies or on our food, like shower gel, hand lotion, and ketchup.

So what are slimes? What are gels, lotions, pastes, oils, greases, syrups, gunks, and goos? What are the special features of all these slimy substances, and why do we love some and hate others?

This "slimy" section lets you investigate the slippery, sticky world of slimes. You can find out what makes a slime, how to measure sliminess in various ways, and how to make slimes thicker and more gooey, or thinner and more runny.

To do the experiments, you'll need to collect many kinds of slimy and gooey substances. There are plenty of ideas on page 38.

For other experiments, you'll need some white plates, a clock or watch that shows minutes, a ruler or measuring tape, cotton thread, some spoons, and a large pitcher. And don't forget to keep the results of your experiments in a special notebook.

SLIMES ON PLATES AND IN NATURE

All around the natural world, there are slimes of many kinds. They are in the inside and on the outside of plants and animals. We know some of these well because they are our foods. Some slimes are used for protection, and to make things slippery or sticky.

Animal slimes are often the ones that some people dislike most. Yet the human body has its own slimes. When it has a cold, it has to blow the slime or mucus out of its nose. It has slimy saliva (spit) in its mouth.

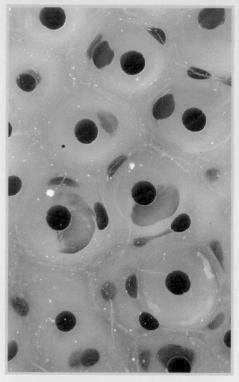

British physicist George Stokes (1819–1903) worked in the branch of science called fluid dynamics. Stokes's law lets you calculate the speed of a ball-shaped object falling through a fluid (liquid or gas), depending on the fluid's viscosity (thickness or runniness, see page 43). Useful, for example, for meteorites and space capsules coming down to Earth!

Experiment 29
Choose your slimes!

Gather a selection of safe substances that are slimy or gooey. There are lots of ideas here, and on page 38. READ THE WARNING on page 38.

1 Look at cosmetics, and products for skin and hair care. They are made to be safe, but only when used properly according to the instructions on the container.

2 The kitchen's a great place to look. Ketchup, mayonnaise, and relish that you pour over food are another good source. Try vegetables or fruit such as mashed banana, too.

3 Some foods seem slimy, greasy, or oily—at least, to some people. You can find out more about them in EXPERIMENT 49.

4 Cooking ingredients are another good idea, like oil, margarine, shortening, and similar greasy substances.

Experiment 30
How runny are slimes?

One of the main features of any slime is its runniness or consistency. Is it thin, watery, and sloppy, or thick and difficult to stir or pour? This feature is called viscosity.

1 You need a selection of slimes, a ruler, a watch or clock, tablespoons, and some white or very pale-colored plates. Those with a perfectly flat central area and a raised rim are best. They can be china or plastic, or even paper.

2 Put a tablespoon-sized drop of slime on the middle of the plate. Start the clock.

3 After a minute, measure the greatest width of the slime patch.

4 Repeat the experiment with other slimes on other plates. The thickest, or most viscous, slimes spread out slowly, if at all. The thinnest, or least viscous, slimes run and spread out fast.

5 After one hour, measure the widths of the patches again. Are the slimes with high viscosity still their original size? Have others, with low viscosity, spread out to cover the whole plate? (Find out more about viscosity in EXPERIMENT 37.)

Viscous, or not?

Viscosity is a proper scientific feature of fluids. Officially, it is a fluid's "resistance to flow." We usually call it thickness or runniness.

- Thick or stiff fluids like molasses and axle grease have high viscosity. They tend not to spread out or run. It's hard to make things move through them. Imagine swimming through syrup!
- Thin or runny liquids like water and milk have low viscosity. They spread out easily, and things can move through them without difficulty.
- "Fluids" include both liquids and gases. So gases, like oxygen in the air around us, have viscosity, too. They are extremely thin and runny!
- Sometimes viscosity changes under pressure. Butter is normally extremely viscous and blob-like. But press it with a spoon or knife, and its viscosity decreases. It becomes slightly more runny. This is how you spread it on bread!

GREAT SLIMERS OF HISTORY

Blaise Pascal (1623–1662), French mathematician and scientific thinker, has a law and a unit named after him. Pascal's law describes how, when you squeeze a liquid such as a slime, the pressure is spread equally all through it. The scientific unit, the pascal, measures pressure.

Experiment 31
How sticky are slimes?

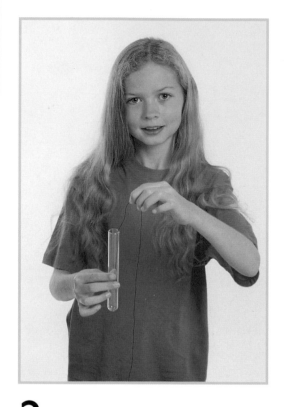

Some slimes spread out, but they don't stick to the things they touch. You can scoop them up and take them away, and they leave no trace. Others are very sticky. They attach or adhere to whatever they touch. This is called adhesion. The best slimes for doing this are glues—also called adhesives!

1 You need a selection of slimes, cotton thread, and test tubes from a science kit, or tall, thin vases.

2 Put a 20 in. (50 cm) length of thread into each test tube, leaving part of it dangling over the side.

3 Pour one of the slimes into a tube so the tube is almost full.

4 Hold the free end of the thread. Slowly and gently, pull it upward. Does the slime stick to the thread and pull up with it? Then the slime is very adhesive or sticky. It may even lift the whole test tube as well!

5 If the slime is not adhesive, the thread slips easily out of it. There are hardly any traces of slime on the thread.

6 Now test each of the other slimes in the same way and make a record in your notebook of how adhesive each slime is.

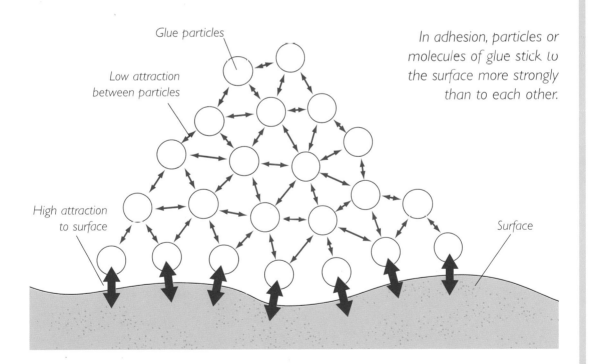

Glue particles

Low attraction between particles

High attraction to surface

In adhesion, particles or molecules of glue stick to the surface more strongly than to each other.

Surface

Adhesion

Adhesion is when something sticks to something else. Glues do this well. The tiny particles or molecules of glue find their way into every crack and crevice, and strongly attract or pull on the thing being glued.

Experiment 32
How stringy are slimes?

Some slimes are very "stringy." When you stretch them, they form long stringy bits. This is called high cohesion. Honey and syrup are good examples. Other slimes can't be pulled in this way. They stay as blobs or the stringy bits soon break. This is low cohesion.

1 You need a selection of slimes (mainly thin or runny ones), some tablespoons, a ruler, and the plates as in EXPERIMENT 30.

2 Scoop up a spoonful of slime. Hold it just above the middle of the plate.

3 Tilt the spoon so the slime oozes over onto the plate.

4 Make the spoon level again, so the slime stops running but stays touching the spoon. Slowly lift it away from the plate.

5 Does the slime stretch and pull easily into stringy bits? This means it is very cohesive. Measure the longest strings with the ruler.

6 If the slime breaks or snaps, it is not cohesive.

Cohesion
Cohesion is when something sticks to itself. Its tiny particles or molecules pull each other much more than they attract other substances. Cohesive things tend to stay in one lump.

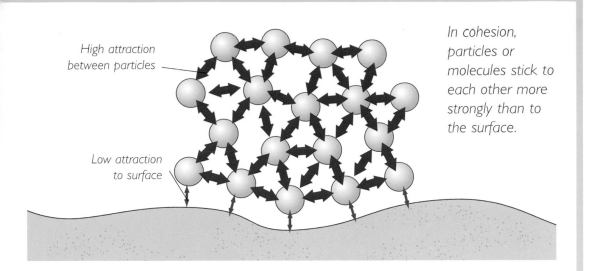

High attraction
between particles

Low attraction
to surface

In cohesion, particles or molecules stick to each other more strongly than to the surface.

Experiment 33
How creepy are slimes?

Slimes have features such as runniness or viscosity, stickiness or adhesion, and stringiness or cohesion. This experiment tests all these features together, to see if slimes can ooze, slide, and creep down a slope.

1 You need a selection of slimes (mainly thin or runny ones), some tablespoons, a watch or clock, and the plates as in EXPERIMENT 30.

2 Scoop a spoonful of slime onto the edge of the plate.

3 Quickly turn the plate up with one side touching the table, and the patch of slime at the top, and start the clock. How long does the slime take to ooze and creep down the plate to reach the table?

4 The creepiest slime takes the shortest time. Some un-creepy slimes may never reach the table. You have to give up with tired arms and boredom!

5 You could have slime races with a friend. Choose a slime each, and do steps 1 to 3 above. Whose slime reaches the table first?

HOW SLIMES CHANGE

Some people like gravy on their food, when it's hot and just poured, and tasty. Delicious! But after half an hour, when the gravy has cooled, it becomes gooey and slimy, and not very appetizing. Yuk! This shows how slimes can change with changing conditions, especially temperature.

Experiment 34
Do slimes dry out?

1 You need a selection of slimes and small white dishes, plus a dishtowel or paper towel.

2 Follow steps 1 and 2 in EXPERIMENT 30. Then cover the slimes with the dishtowel or paper towel, to stop things like dust or flies from landing on them. Leave the slimes in a safe, warm place. Check with an adult.

3 Look at them again the next day, and then after two days. Some may have dried out partly, into a sticky goo. Some dry out completely, into a hard crust or powder. Others resist drying out. They are still slimy. Can you understand how this feature fits with the use of each slime?

4 Don't forget to dispose of these old, dried slimes properly before they become moldy. Check with an adult.

Experiment 35
Slimes and cold

Cold makes most things shrink. It also makes many slimes thicker and more viscous. Painters know that in winter, paint is harder to spread with a brush.

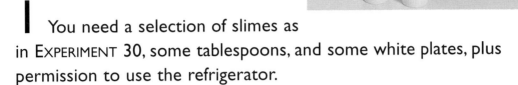

1 You need a selection of slimes as in EXPERIMENT 30, some tablespoons, and some white plates, plus permission to use the refrigerator.

2 Put your slimes in the refrigerator for an hour. Take them out, and before they warm up, carry out the runniness test as in steps 2, 3, and 4 for EXPERIMENT 30.

3 Test the time each cold slime takes to spread compared to when it was at room temperature (see EXPERIMENT 30). Do most slimes become thicker when they are cold?

Experiment 36
Slimes and warmth

Warmth makes most things expand. It also makes many slimes thinner and less viscous. Chocolate is hard at room temperature, but if it gets warm, it melts.

1 Use the same materials as for step 1 of EXPERIMENT 35. Put the slimes in a warm place for an hour.

2 Before they cool, do the runniness test as in EXPERIMENT 30.

3 Test the time each warm slime takes to spread out and its size as compared to when it was at room temperature. Do most slimes become thinner when they are hot?

MEASURING SLIMES

Some people spend years measuring slimes, goos, gels, and similar substances. They want to know how fast slimes run and how easy they are to pour. They test 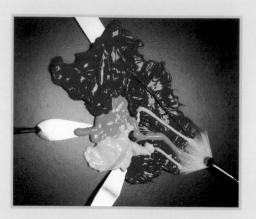 and check features like viscosity, adhesion, cohesion, and changes with warmth and cold. These people are carrying out research into a huge variety of products, from sauces and ketchups, to paints and lubricating oils.

Experiment 37
Making a slimometer

Try making an easy-to-use gadget for measuring slimes. It mainly detects viscosity or runniness, and lets you compare the viscosities of various slimes. It can be used for lots of the experiments in this section of the book.

1 You need a watch or clock, two see-through test tubes, or tall thin beakers, or similar items, so that one fits neatly inside the other. (Try educational suppliers or science stores.) This is your "slimometer." Make a stand from strong card and tape, to hold the tubes safely upright.

2 Begin with a runny slime, like shampoo. Half-fill the slimometer's wider, outer tube with it.

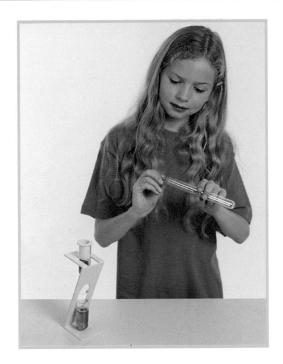

3 Hold the inner tube in the outer tube, so its base is just above the slime's surface.

4 Let the inner tube go. It should sink down into the slime. Time it, from when you let it go, to when it stops sinking and reaches the bottom. This is the sinking time. Make a note of this.

5 If the inner tube doesn't sink, the slime is quite thick. Make the inner tube heavier by putting in a weight such as a ball of modeling clay.

6 If the inner tube still doesn't sink, add another same-sized clay ball to make it even heavier, and so on. Record the final sinking time and the number of balls in your notebook (see page 52).

Scientific slimometers

There are various designs of real slimometers, used in science laboratories and research centers. They are called viscometers because they usually measure viscosity.

One type is called the Ostwald viscometer, named after Friedrich Ostwald (see EXPERIMENT 47). It measures the time taken for a slime or liquid to run down the inside of a very thin tube, called a capillary tube. Another type measures how fast a heavy ball falls through a slime or liquid. A similar but homemade slimometer is shown on the right.

Experiment 38
Comparing slimes

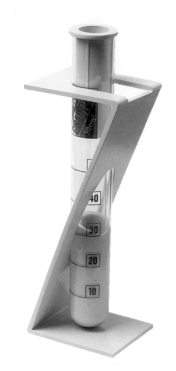

Following on from EXPERIMENT 37, test lots of different slimes with the slimometer. Some may be so thick that the inner tube does not sink into them, even with all the clay balls inside. In this case you could try extra weights, such as marbles. Wash and dry the slimometer after each experiment.

1 You are now ready to compare the slimes. Sort them into groups according to the number of balls needed in the inner tube.

2 In each group, the slime with the quickest sinking time is first.

3 Now add all the groups together into one long list in your notebook. At the top of the list is the slime which needed the fewest balls in the inner tube and had the fastest sinking time. This is the thinnest, runniest, or least viscous slime.

4 At the bottom of the list is the slime which needed most balls in the inner tube, and had the slowest sinking time. This is the thickest or most viscous slime.

5 Are the slimes in the order you expected? Maybe a slime that seems thin and runny comes low on the list. Do colors make any difference? Copy the chart below into your notebook and complete it using the results of your experiments.

	Number of balls	Sinking time
Slime 1		
Slime 2		
Slime 3		
Slime 4		

Experiment 39
Pouring slimes

The ability to pour certain slimy substances, like sauce and gel, is **VERY** important. Pourability depends partly on viscosity. Too thick, and your favorite sauce stays stuck in its bottle. Too thin, and it floods out all over your food! Manufacturers spend millions on getting the right runniness in their products.

1 You need some test tubes or tall thin containers, and a watch to measure seconds and minutes, plus a large piece of card, a pen, and a bowl, and a selection of fairly thin slimes such as baby oil, fruit juice, barbecue sauce, and shampoo. Use some of the same slimes as in EXPERIMENT 38.

2 Draw a line near the top of the card. It should be at an angle of about 30° to horizontal, as shown below.

3 Fill each test tube or similar container with a slimy substance.

4 Hold this test tube or container by its neck, above the bowl. Hold the card near it, with the line at the top. Get the watch ready.

5 Pour the slime into the bowl. As you tilt the tube, start the watch. Make sure you keep the tube at the same angle as the line.

6 Time how long the slime takes to pour out of the tube, until it begins to drip slowly, less than one drip each minute. Record the result in your notebook.

horizontal

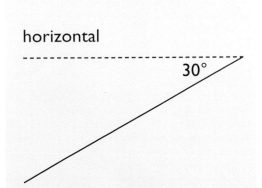

7 Test the other slimes in the same way. Which pours fastest, and which is slowest? Make a list in your notebook, from the fastest pourer to the slowest.

53

Experiment 40
Checking up on slimes

Not all science involves doing experiments. Sometimes you can gain understanding simply by thinking, writing notes, and having ideas. This is called "armchair science." Some of the greatest scientific advances have been made in this way.

1 Look at the results of the previous experiments in your notebook. Check the list from EXPERIMENT 38, comparing viscosity, with the list from EXPERIMENT 39 comparing pourability.

2 Are the lists broadly the same? A slime which is thin and runny should pour out of its container faster.

3 If you were inventing a new kind of ketchup, where would it come on the list? What about a new type of shower gel?

Experiment 41
Making powdered slime

1 You need "dry slime" powder, designed to mix with water to make a slime, available from most toy and hobby stores. Follow the instructions.

2 Or stir some wallpaper paste powder or granules with a little water in a cup. Add a little more water each time.

3 Your slime should soon be ready. Remember to put the "dry slime" slime back into its container after use.

Scotsman James Clerk Maxwell (1831–1879) was one of the greatest "armchair scientists." He did some experiments, but his greatest achievements were with pencil and paper. He described how air and gases, as well as slimes and other liquids, have viscosity. He also showed that light rays were part of a whole set of rays and waves called the electromagnetic spectrum. This helped in the invention of radio.

Experiment 42
Are watery slimes less slimy?

Adding water to a slime can make it thinner and more runny if the substance can be dissolved in water. Gelatins, such as Jell-o, are specially made to do this.

1 You need three similar gelatins to make up, plus an adult to do all the cooking, various spoons, and several bowls.

2 Read the instructions on the pack. Make one gelatin, using the amount of water advised.

3 Make a second gelatin in the same way, but use half of the water advised.

4 Make a third gelatin using twice the water advised.

5 Put the gelatins aside to cool and then compare them. Have they all set? Which is thickest? Does the third gelatin set at all, or stay as a runny slime? It seems that more water means more runny!

6 Now repeat the experiment using wallpaper paste.

Experiment 43
Dissolving slimes

Most slimes are based on a liquid which is made thicker by dissolving substances in it. Common household slimes have water as their main liquid. Water is called the solvent. The slimes in garages and factories may be based on different, more dangerous, solvents, such as gasoline or alcohol.

1 Choose a dry substance that is made into a slime by mixing it with water. You also need other liquids, such as milk and vinegar.

2 Make up one tablespoon of the dry substance with water. Next mix tablespoons of the substance with each of the other liquids.

3 Compare the results and record them in your notebook. Does the wrong solvent have much effect?

Experiment 44
Absorbing slimes

Do slimes soak into certain substances or surfaces? Could an object soak up or absorb a thin slime as easily as a thick one? In this experiment, you can find out what you should use to mop up a slime fastest.

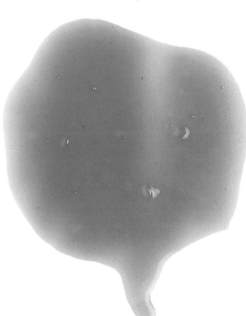

1 You need a plentiful slimy substance such as thick liquid detergent, a tablespoon, and a selection of various objects with different types of surfaces. Try a shiny china plate, blotting paper, an old duster, a paper towel, an old glossy magazine, an old newspaper, and so on.

2 Put the objects in a row on the table. Pour a tablespoon of slime onto each one.

3 Watch the slime and see how it spreads out, and perhaps gets absorbed. Which substance or surface soaks up slime fastest?

4 You could try the same experiment with other slimes of different runniness. Are the thickest or most viscous slimes the slowest to be absorbed?

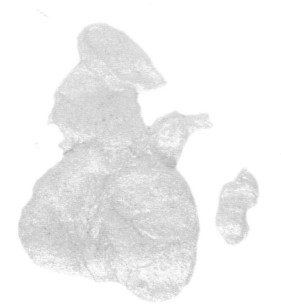

Experiment 45
Filtering slimes

Some slimes are clear and see-through, even though they may be colored. Others are not. This experiment tests whether goos, gels, and slimes contain particles of any kind. It works best with thin and runny substances.

1 You need a selection of very thin and runny and preferably colored slimes, a clock or watch, kitchen funnel, a clear glass or plastic pitcher with a fairly narrow neck, and blotting paper cut with care into circular shapes.

2 Put the funnel in the neck of the pitcher. Fold the blotting paper to make a cone shape and fit it into the funnel. Get the watch ready.

3 Pour the slime quickly to almost fill the funnel. Time how long it takes the slime to filter and drip through the paper.

4 Compare the filtered slime to what is left behind on the paper. Are there tiny particles, or any colored substances?

Experiment 46
Colors of slimes

Why are some gooey and slimy substances colored? Perhaps it is to look nice, as with shower gels, or to be useful, as with pastes. Some are simply their natural colors, like certain sauces and food dressings.

1 You need a selection of colorful slimes, like bath or shower gel, liquid detergent, skin cream, and a paint of some type, such as a tube of artist's oil paint, plus a tablespoon and an old magazine with very shiny, glossy pages.

2 Tear some pages out of the magazine which are similar in appearance, with about the same amounts of writing and pictures.

3 Put a tablespoon of one slime onto the center of a page Spread out the slime as evenly as you can, using the spoon, or perhaps a small paintbrush or plastic spatula.

4 Quickly repeat this for each slime, cleaning the spoon each time.

5 Look at your magazine pages and compare them. Can you still see the words and pictures through some of the spread-out slimes? Which slimy substance has the strongest or densest color, and the best covering power? Should the paint give the best coverage? After all, it's made for that job!

Experiment 47
Slimes in pipes

Slimes sometimes get stuck. Runny liquids like water flow easily through small pipes and thin tubes. But slimes are usually thicker and more viscous, and they can't flow so easily. The scientific gadget called an Ostwald viscometer measures how fast (or slow) slimes flow.

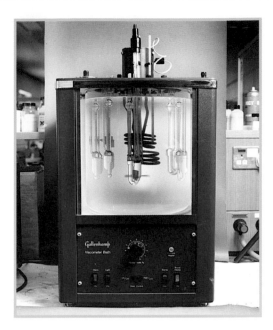

1 Choose a fairly thick slime, such as ketchup. You also need a watch or clock, and a selection of tube-like or pipe-like containers such as a wide-mouthed jar and a narrow jar, and a teaspoon.

2 Fill the widest of your containers half-full of slime. Then turn it upside-down! Make sure it doesn't make a mess by putting the whole experiment on a newspaper.

3 Start the clock and see how long the slime takes to slide or slip or drip out. Record the time in your notebook.

4 Do the same for the next narrowest container, and so on.

5 Does the slime take longer to come out of wide pipes and tubes, or narrow ones? With a very narrow container and a very thick slime, it may take days to fall out!

GREAT SLIMERS OF HISTORY

French scientist Jean Poiseulle (1797–1869) described how liquids such as slimes, and gases, too, flow through pipes and tubes. His work is used by designers of water faucets, plumbing systems, jet engines, and hydroelectric power stations!

Why are some plants slimy?

The slimy parts of a plant are usually its fruits. They are full of a soft fleshy substance. Why? Usually, to attract hungry animals, who eat the fruits. In the fruit is the plant's hard, tough seed or pit. The seeds pass through the intestinal tract of the animal and come out the other end, far from the parent plant. This helps plants to spread their seeds.

Another slimy part of many plants is the sap. This can be compared to a plant's blood. It's a thick liquid, rich in sugars and minerals. Sap is made in the leaves and flows through tubes within the plant, carrying nourishment to all its parts.

The sap and resin from trees is harnessed by people for many different purposes. Resin from the pine tree has been used as glue for hundreds of years. Amber, the fossilized tree resin from conifers, is used as an attractive, decorative stone in jewelry.

Rubber

Rubber is a gum extracted from tropical trees. Its molecules have twists and loops in them which make rubber more elastic. The molecules in raw rubber are not linked, and the rubber itself is therefore weak. When rubber is heated with sulfur, its molecules link. This makes it stronger and increases its elasticity.

Maple syrup

The sugar maple tree of North America produces a sap which is tapped. This sap is then processed so that it is between 30 and 50 times more concentrated than the sap itself. This sweet-tasting syrup is used on pancakes.

Experiment 48
Turn an egg into slime!

Many animals, such as insects, fish, frogs, and birds, lay eggs. And many of these have a slimy white or a gooey yolk inside. We use chicken eggs as food, so they are a good natural thing to test.

1 You'll need a chicken egg, and some soy sauce used for food flavoring, plus cooking utensils, and an adult to supervise.

2 Crack the egg and separate the yolk from the white.

3 Put the yolk in a cup and stir it gently with a spoon.

4 Add a few drops of soy sauce to the egg yolk and stir gently. Add a few more drops, and stir again. Gradually the runny egg yolk turns into a thick, blobby, sticky, brown goo! Can you stir it to get rid of the lumps?

5 Why does this happen? Natural food chemicals called alkaloids in the soy sauce react with proteins in the egg yolk. The proteins lose their smooth texture and clump together—this is called denaturing. The same happens with heat when you fry an egg.

GREAT SLIMERS OF HISTORY

Charles Cross (1855–1935), an English chemist, discovered the viscose process for making artificial fibers such as rayon. Wood pulp is mixed with various chemicals, turned into the brown slime called viscose, and then squirted through tiny holes to make the rayon strands.

Experiment 49
Plant slimes

Test the sliminess of different plant foods on your friends. Some people may like them; others hate the slippery, sticky, gooey feeling and texture!

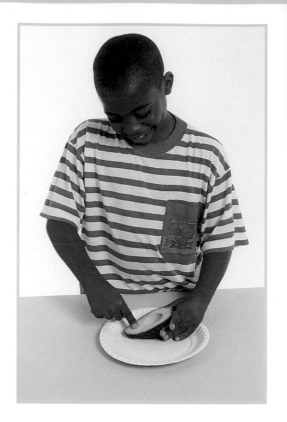

1 You need a selection of plant foods—fruits and vegetables, such as grapes, avocado, litchi nuts, okra, olives, ripe pears and plums, and a banana. You will also need a fork, plates, and an adult with a knife to help.

2 Ask the adult to cut open the foods. Feel the "flesh," the soft edible parts inside. Are they slippery, squishy, sloppy, or slimy in any way?

3 Cut out the fleshy bits of each food in turn and mash them on a plate. Make them into a soft pulp. Is it slimy now?

4 Ask your friends to vote for the slimiest food. Which one wins? Would you eat it?

Muddy slimes

Do you remember your last visit to a muddy place? It might be the backyard, park, river bank, lakeside, marsh, or beach. Some kinds of muddy and sandy substances feel slimy. This is often due to dead, decaying remains of plants and animals in the substance. It's also due to the worms, snails, and similar animals that live in the mud, who eat all the rotting stuff, and make slime to protect themselves.

Next time you go to one of these places, test the sliminess of the mud with a shoe or stick.

Howver, be VERY careful.

Slimy mud can be smelly, soft, sticky—and can even suck you under.

Experiment 50
Animal slimes

Most people have encountered slimy animals. They may shudder and go "uurgh!" The creatures would probably do the same if they could, as people touch them. Yet some animals have an unfair reputation for being slippery and slimy.

1 Collect a couple of slimy animals from a park or backyard. You could try a slug, snail, or worm.

2 Make them feel at home. Put some moist soil, leaves, and twigs in a plastic carton or box. Cut small holes in the lid to let air in.

3 Watch these creatures as they move. See how a slug or snail leaves a trail of slime, or mucus, as it glides along. The mucus helps it to grip smooth surfaces like shiny tree bark, glossy leaves, and also plastic cartons, painted wood, and glass windows.

4 Always return these animals to the place where you found them, within a few hours.

5 Think of creatures which are supposed to be slimy— maybe an eel, frog, toad, newt, lizard, or snake. Perhaps friends have one or more as pets. Ask if you can touch them safely. Which ones are truly slimy?

Pythons can reach a length of over 20 feet (6 meters) and kill their prey by constriction (crushing). Contrary to popular belief, however, snakes are not slimy to the touch!

INTRODUCING SMELL

Every day, you smell things with your nose—from lovely foods and scented flowers, to choking car exhaust fumes and foul toilets. Even "fresh air" has its own special odor.

We use our sense of smell in all kinds of important ways—it helps us detect a rotten egg at the back of the refrigerator and warns us if our home is on fire. Yet, however amazing our sense of smell is, it is only a fraction as powerful as that of many other animals. A polar bear, for example, can smell a dead sea lion 3 miles (4.8 kilometers) away.

Smells, stinks, stenches, odors, and whiffs are in themselves puzzling. We can't see them or sense them in any other way, except with our noses. Unlike light and sound, smells are not easily detected by machines. There are cameras for light, and microphones for sound, but there are very few gadgets that can detect or measure smells.

In fact, we don't really know exactly how the human nose works! Smells are very personal—we all have our own likes and dislikes. This is what makes smell so fascinating and mysterious. Your notebook will make interesting reading!

THE SENSE OF SMELL

The human body has five main senses. These are sight, hearing, touch, taste—and smell. Most people use sight as the main sense, and perhaps smell is the least

obvious sense. In fact, we often use several senses at the same time to build up an overall impression of something. When you sit down to eat a meal, your eyes see it, and of course your nose smells it. But your ears may hear it sizzling or being cut, and as your tongue tastes it, your mouth also feels its temperature, hardness, and texture.

Using all these senses, it's usually easy to identify what you're eating. But take away the senses and the clues they give you, one by one, and it becomes much more difficult! EXPERIMENTS 51 to 55 show this process in action.

Your sense of smell comes from two

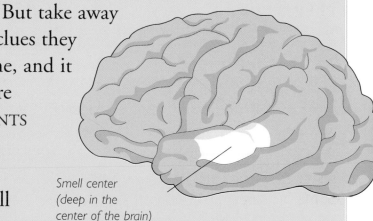

Smell center
(deep in the
center of the brain)

olfactory patches in the roof of your nasal cavity—the hollow chamber just behind your nose. Each patch is about as big as a thumbnail and contains 10 million microscopic smelling cells. As you breathe, air carrying tiny, floating smell particles called *odorants* comes in through the nostrils and swirls around the cavity. The odorant particles land on the smelling cells and make them produce nerve signals. These signals go along nerves to the smell center in the brain where they are identified.

Experiment 51
Sight, touch, and smell

You can test how the senses work together by asking some friends to identify pieces of common foods. See how easy this is, using clues from sight such as shape and color, clues from touch like hardness and texture, and of course smell—but no taste.

1 Choose a selection of food items you can peel and divide up easily, such as a lemon, apple, banana, potato, and orange.

2 Peel the foods, or ask an adult to cut off the skins. Put them in separate dishes.

3 Ask a friend to come into the room and identify the pieces of food, without tasting. Watch carefully to see how she or he looks, touches, and perhaps sniffs the foods.

4 How many items were correctly identified? Copy the chart below into your notebook and fill in the results of EXPERIMENTS 51 to 55. Most people rely on the sight of the food—its color, size, shape, and surface appearance—as well as touching it, to identify it. Smell may help, but it isn't the main sense.

Food	Experiments				
	1	2	3	4	5
Onion	✔				
Lemon	✔				
Apple	✔				
Banana	✔				

✔ = identified correctly
✘ = not identified correctly

Experiment 52
Touch and smell

Following EXPERIMENT 51, you can remove the clues that eyes provide about the identity of food. Now there's only smell and touch.

1 Do steps 1 and 2 of EXPERIMENT 51.

2 Ask a friend to identify the foods without tasting or seeing them, either. He or she should wear a blindfold. Help your friend find the dishes.

3 Watch to see how your friend behaves. She or he will probably touch and press the foods, and also sniff them much more thoroughly, to help identification.

4 How many correct scores are there? Without sight, most people spend more time touching and smelling the food.

Experiment 53
Less touch, more smell

After EXPERIMENTS 51 and 52, you can now remove some of the clues that touch provides about the identity of food. As there's less touch—and still no taste—smell becomes more important.

1 Follow steps 1 and 2 as described for EXPERIMENT 51. This time, make touch give less information by asking an adult to slice each food item into small equal-sized cubes.

2 Ask a friend to identify the foods without tasting or seeing them. He or she should wear a blindfold.

3 Watch to see how your friend behaves. She or he will probably touch and press the foods even more, and also sniff them even more thoroughly, to help identification.

4 How many correct scores are there? Record the results in your notebook. Without sight, and with fewer clues from touch, most people spend more time smelling the food.

Experiment 54
Even less touch, more smell

Now it's time to remove even more clues from touch. To do this, mash each food into a soft pulp with a pestle and mortar. This gets rid of all the information you can feel about hardness and texture.

1 Follow step 1 as described for EXPERIMENT 53. But make touch give even less information by mashing each food into a soft pulp.

2 Ask a friend to identify the foods without tasting or seeing them. He or she should wear a blindfold. Help your friend find the dishes.

3 Watch to see how your friend behaves. She or he will probably feel the foods, but get little idea from touch. So sniffing and smelling become even more important for identification.

4 Record the results in your notebook. Without sight, and with hardly any clues from touch, people spend even more time smelling the food.

Shark attack!
Sharks have a very good sense of smell. They can smell blood in the water from more than 1 mile (1.6 kilometres) away.

Experiment 55
Smell alone

This is the last in the series of five experiments. The only way to identify the food now is by smell. This makes it more difficult. An added problem is that when we eat, what we experience as "smell" is a combination of information from smell and taste. Smell alone gives much less information.

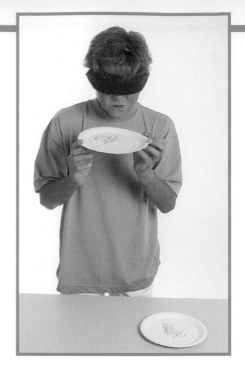

1 Follow steps 1 and 2 as for EXPERIMENT 54, mashing the food into pulp. Your friend wears a blindfold and now is not allowed to touch the food either.

2 The sense of smell is the only clue to identification. Your friend may spend a long time sniffing the odors and trying to guess what the food is.

3 How many correct scores are there? Record the results in your notebook. Without sight, touch, or taste, identifying foods from smell alone can be very difficult!

Experiment 56
Smell with your mouth!

Your nose detects tiny odorant particles floating in the air. They usually get into the nasal cavity through the nostrils, in breathed-in air. But that's not the only way. There's another route into the nasal cavity, which air follows as you breathe in and out through your nose. It's around the rear of the palate, the shelf which forms the roof of the mouth and the floor of the nasal cavity. Sometimes smells can drift in through the mouth and then up around the palate, to be detected in the nasal cavity.

1 You need a clothespin and something strong-smelling, like an onion.

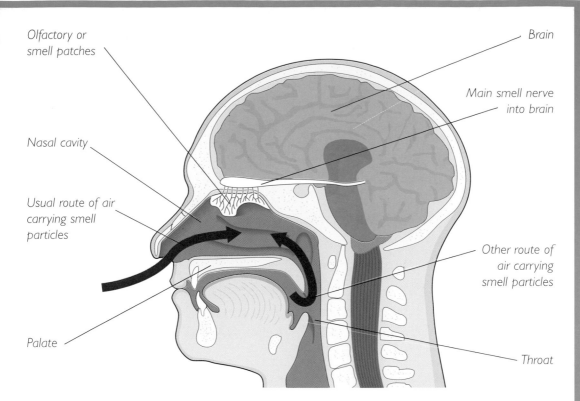

Olfactory or
smell patches

Brain

Main smell nerve
into brain

Nasal cavity

Usual route of air
carrying smell
particles

Other route of
air carrying
smell particles

Palate

Throat

2 Put the clothespin carefully over your nose. Make sure that you can breathe easily through your mouth.

3 Ask an adult to cut an onion open. Breathe near it, in and out through your mouth.

4 Can you smell the onion, even though your nose is closed? The smell wafts in through your mouth, around the palate, and up into the nasal cavity. This is also how you get the smells of different food as you are chewing and eating them.

STRENGTHS OF SMELLS

Have you ever smelled a really strong odor? Some smells are so powerful that they make your nose wrinkle, your eyes water, and your throat cough.

Other odors are faint and fleeting—you think you can detect them, but you're not quite sure, and then they're gone. The strength of a smell depends on the nature of the substance itself, and also on how much there is in the form of floating odorant particles.

Experiment 57
How faint can smells be?

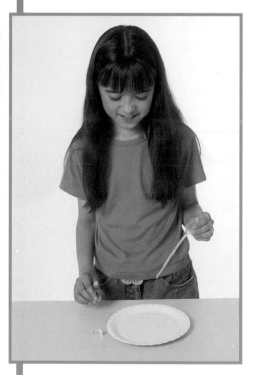

Using small droppers, such as eye or ear droppers, you can find out how little of a smelly substance is needed for you to detect it. The amounts vary enormously, from a tiny drop to a whole roomful. Many things have no smell at all!

1 Choose a pleasantly scented substance such as a shower gel. You will need a friend, but do not tell him or her the identity of the scent.

2 In another room, place one drop of the substance on a clean dish. Ask your friend to go into the room and smell hard from a distance of 1 yard (0.9 meters), allowing a few seconds for the smell to spread.

3 Can your friend smell anything at all? If so, can he or she guess what it is, or at least, guess the type of smell?

4 If not, repeat step 2, but use two drops of the substance. Keep doing this until your friend can identify the substance.

5 Try other substances with different types of smell. Which is strongest? That is, which can your friend smell from the least number of drops? Wash your hands after testing each substance.

The emperor moth

The emperor moth has the most sensitive "nose" of any creature. When looking for a mate, the female releases her scent in the wind. The male moth's sensitive antennae can pick up just one molecule of the female's scent from as far as 3 miles (4.8 kilometres) away.

Experiment 58
Which smell is strongest?

This experiment continues from the previous one. It compares the same amounts—the same number of drops—of various smelly substances, to see which one has the strongest effect on the human nose.

1 Collect a selection of scented liquids as for EXPERIMENT 57, such as perfume, aftershave, disinfectant, orange juice, and soy sauce.

2 Repeat steps 1 and 2 from EXPERIMENT 57. Test the substances in turn, using five drops each time. Remember to wash your hands.

3 Each time, ask your friend to give the smell a number between 1 and 5 which indicates how strong it is—a very powerful smell could score 5. Identifying the smell isn't as important as testing the effect of its strength.

4 Compare the results. Which smell seemed the strongest? Often sweet and pleasant smells seem less powerful than the sour or bitter ones which make your nose wrinkle.

Experiment 59
Confusing smells

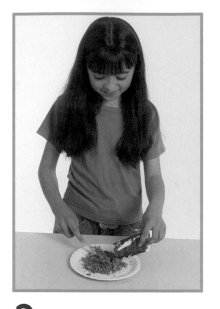

You can confuse the senses and trick a friend by making a food that smells like one thing, but tastes like another. This means it's doubly difficult to identify!

1 Ask an adult to make some mashed potatoes with nothing added, or borrow a spoonful of mashed potatoes at mealtime!

2 Mix half of the mashed potatoes with an unexpected, strong-smelling substance, such as cocoa powder or lime juice.

3 Blindfold your friend, who has not seen your preparations. Ask her or him to smell the mashed potatoes on its own, identify it, and then eat it to confirm the identification. Smell and taste are confused. Which one "wins"—or is it impossible to identify either?

Experiment 60
Battle of the smells

When two odors meet, which one is strongest? This depends on the nature of the smells, and also on their relative strengths.

1 Collect different smelly substances for this experiment. Try a selection of drinks such as coffee, cola, chocolate milk, mint tea, and fruit juice.

2 Choose two of the substances and call them A and B. Put a little of A into a small sealable container, such as a corked tube, and an equal amount of B in another. Close or seal the containers.

3 Ask a friend to stand at an equal distance from each container with his or her eyes closed. Open both containers together, leave them open for two seconds, then close them again.

4 Your friend should now try to identify the strongest smell. Record the two smells and which one "won" in your notebook. Pair each smell in turn with all the others. Which smell is the strongest?

Experiment 61
Why smells fade

Walk into an indoor swimming pool and you can smell the odor of chemicals. But 20 minutes later, do you still notice it? A new smell seems strong and clear when you first detect it, but it soon appears to fade, and you notice it less. This happens even if the odorant particles of the smell remain as numerous in the air. This fading with time is called habituation. It affects other senses, too, especially touch.

1 Choose a strong, nice smell such as a newly opened pine air freshener. Take it into a room where there are no other smells.

2 Sit next to the air freshener and sniff hard. Can you smell it? Wait five minutes and then see if you can still detect the scent. Is it still as strong?

3 After another five minutes, do the same. The smell will probably seem weaker, and you may not even notice it. The smell is still there, but your own nose has almost stopped detecting it. There are many smells in normal air. Without habituation, you'd continually be detecting all of them. Habituation allows us to notice mainly new smells, or when a smell changes in strength.

GREAT STINKERS OF HISTORY

Swedish chemist Carl Wilhelm Scheele (1742–1786) was the first person to make the very strong, poisonous, greenish gas called chlorine. In its pure form, it has an extremely choking smell and can easily kill animals and people. Some cleansers, bleaches, and swimming pools have very faint traces of chlorine smell.

Experiment 62
Releasing smells

You can test how cutting, squeezing, and mashing something can make its smell more powerful. You need to get out, or extract, from foods, flowers, or herbs their smelly substances—called the aromatic essences.

1 Choose a nice-smelling object like a fresh flower, such as a scented rose.

2 Smell it carefully from different distances, and get friends to do the same. Record your impressions of how strong its smell is, and how sweet.

3 Ask an adult to cut it into pieces, then mash these with warm water in a grinder, masher, or pestle and mortar. Does the scent smell stronger as you do this?

4 Pour the mashed-up matter through tissue paper lining a funnel. Let the water drip into a container, while the solid parts stay in the paper.

GREAT STINKERS OF HISTORY

The Ancient Egyptians made perfumes over three thousand years ago. The Persians carried on this tradition. In Europe, the first specially-made perfume that we know about was "Hungary Water." It was mixed for Queen Elizabeth of Hungary in about 1370. Before this, people of the time used fresh flowers and herbs to mask the nasty odors of their unwashed medieval homes, clothes, and bodies. Elizabeth's Hungary Water was the beginning of the huge modern perfume-making industry.

5 Sniff the solid matter in the paper. Compare it with the liquid which passed through into the container. Which has captured the essential smell of the original flower? Does this show that the smelly substance dissolves in water?

Experiment 63
Smells that make you cry

Some smells are so strong, they make your eyes water. Peeling onions is probably the best known. Why does it happen, and can you stop it?

1 Peel an onion and then ask an adult to carefully slice it with a safely blunt knife. It smells strong, but do their eyes water? Probably! This is due to chemicals called cepiates, which are odorants given off into the air as the onion's flesh is cut.

2 Besides affecting your nose, the cepiates land on the delicate coverings of your eyes, called the conjunctivas, and that stings!

3 Peel another onion, but do it from the "top," or stem end, first. This means you peel and cut the lower or root part last. Is the smell concentrated in the root?

4 Peel a third onion—under water. The water absorbs most of the odorant. Your eyes are less likely to water. Relief at last!

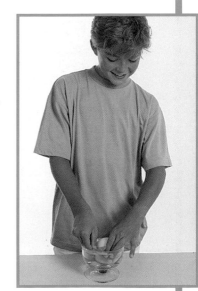

NICE 'N' NASTY SMELLS

Smell is a very personal sense. We all have our smelly likes and dislikes. Some people adore the aroma of asparagus cooking and the scent of soap, while others loathe them. Almost everyone turns up their nose at smells such as dirty socks, car exhaust fumes, and methane gas from rotting plants in a muddy marsh. Yet scents, such as pine and rose, are popular with nearly everyone. Smells can put you in a good mood, bring back memories, and even help you to get better from illness!

Experiment 64
Top of the smells

You can study, in a scientific way, which types of smells are most popular. This research work is carried out by huge organizations when they test new brands of air fresheners, cleansers, and similar products.

1 Gather five or more pleasantly scented substances. You might consider pine air freshener, a piece of fresh-baked bread, a square of chocolate, a scented candle, a slice of lemon, potpourri, and so on.

2 Put a little piece of each into a separate container, like a jar or test tube, and seal it.

3 Cover each container with paper, to hide what's inside. Label them A, B, C, D, and E. Make a secret list of what's in them for you alone!

4 Ask a friend to sniff the containers one by one as you open them for a couple of seconds. The friend doesn't have to identify the smell. He or she simply gives it a score, depending on whether it is pleasant, or not.

5 Ask the friend to give the scores 1 to 5 to the smells, 1 being the most unpleasant, and 5 being the nicest. Record the results in your notebook.

6 Ask several friends to take this smell test. Do most people prefer the same scents, or do they have very different views on what is pleasant or not? Add up the results. Draw a chart showing which smell scores highest.

Experiment 65
The next great chip

You can buy potato chips in all kinds of smells and flavors, such as beef, barbecue, bacon, salt, and even chili. You can also produce your own special chips that smell and taste of very strange things indeed, and test them on friends. Could you invent a chip flavor that will become the next successful fashion?

1 You need adult help for this. Ask the adult to find a recipe for potato chips, and to peel and thin-slice some potatoes according to the recipe.

2 Soak the raw potato slices for an hour in something which is unusual for a potato chip flavor, but safe to eat. You could try cabbage water, beet juice, avocado pulp, minty water, or cherry juice.

3 Follow the recipe and ask an adult to deep-fry the potato slices in the usual way.

4 Test your new chips on volunteers. Ask them to smell the chips first. Do people prefer traditional versions, or do they like the new and unusual ones? Eat them if you dare!

GREAT STINKERS OF HISTORY

French chemist Antoine Lavoisier (1743–1794) discovered the substance sulfur, which has a very strong smell of its own. The characteristic odors of volcano fumes contain sulfur gases, and safe sulfur-containing chemicals are sometimes used on skin ulcers and sores. Iron sulfide is combined with hydrochloric acid to make a gas called hydrogen sulfide—which has the stench of "rotten eggs."

Experiment 66
Not a rotten egg?

One of the worst known smells is rotten eggs. It's based on the gas hydrogen sulfide, which the egg produces as it goes bad. This "egg stink" will certainly surprise your friends!

1 You need adult help for this. Ask the adult to keep some eggs in a warm place, but very safe and out-of-the-way.

2 After a week, ask the adult to crack an egg into a bowl. Do this outdoors. Is the rotten egg smell present?

3 If not, after another week, repeat the test on another egg. How long does it take for the famously awful smell of rotten eggs to develop?

WARNING: Always dispose of rotten eggs properly. They are extremely dangerous if eaten.

4 When it does, put the bowl somewhere out of sight when your friends come around to visit. See if they notice the stink!

Experiment 67
Memories are made of smells

Our memory for smells is very powerful. An odor such as a musty house or a certain cleaning product can conjure up memories after many years.

1 You need adult help for this. Ask the adult to help you choose smelly substances that might remind people of events or places. Consider salty water (for the beach), damp soil (for the backyard or woods), furniture polish (for household chores), and warm milk (for a baby's nighttime drink).

2 Do steps 2, 3, and 4 as described for EXPERIMENT 64. But ask people if the smells bring back memories, and if so, what of?

3 Record the results in your notebook. Do most people link the same smell to the same type of place or event? What's the most distant memory brought back by a smell? Some older people can remember smells from more than 50 years ago!

GREAT STINKERS OF HISTORY

English scientist Humphry Davy (1778–1829) did many experiments on the effects of "laughing gas," a vapor called nitrous oxide. It was used for a time as an anesthetic to put people to sleep during operations. But its harmful effects on the body were soon discovered. Laughing gas is restricted by law and banned for most uses.

Experiment 68
Get-well smells

Many scents and odors are used in medicines—especially when the illness affects the breathing system, including the nose, throat, windpipe, or lungs. Some of these medications give off vapors that help to loosen and dissolve slimy mucus which blocks the nose in a cold, or clogs the throat, lower airways, and lungs in a cough.

1 Ask an adult to help you find at home a selection of over-the-counter medicines and remedies for coughs, colds, sore throats, and similar breathing-type illnesses. They come in many different forms such as pastilles, lozenges, capsules, powders for drinks, sprays, aerosols, syrups, rubs, and drops.

2 Smell each preparation in its raw form, straight from its container. Which is strongest?

3 Ask an adult to help you prepare a few of the remedies, as though you were going to use them. For example, make a soothing sore-throat drink from powder, moisten the lozenge as though it's being chewed, and spread the chest-rub on the back of your hand.

4 Smell them again. Which is strongest now?

5 Look at the variety of remedies and see if certain smells keep cropping up. How about lemon, menthol, orange, eucalyptus, and mint?

WARNING: Never experiment with medicines or take them without proper advice from a doctor or qualified adult.

Aromatherapy

Some people use a type of medicine called aromatherapy. The expert aromatherapist tries to find out what is wrong with a sick person, and advises massage with strong-smelling essential oils. The exact type of oil and its aroma are chosen according to the health problem.

THE SMELL INDUSTRY

Every year, companies spend millions on smells. Some products are specially designed to have certain smells, such as deodorants, odor-eaters, neutralizers, and air fresheners.

Stores may add scents such as fresh-baked bread to their air conditioning to put customers in a happy and hungry mood. Then they buy more! Almost any product, from a book to a car, can have a pleasing odor, even if it's for a boring job, like oven-cleaner or liquid detergent. If it smells good, people are more likely to like it, and buy it!

Experiment 69
"Fresh" air?

You can do a consumer test to find out which deodorant or air freshener is most effective at masking smells. Do "fresh air" air fresheners really make the air smell like it does outside on a clean, clear day— which is probably of nothing at all? Or do they have added perfumes?

I Collect a selection of air fresheners and similar sprays. Taking care to hold each can well away from your face, squirt a one-second blast from each into the air in turn, and sniff its aroma. Allow a minute or two for each smell to fade, then try the next. Which is the most powerful, and which do you prefer?

2 Spray the cans in pairs, two at the same time, for exactly one second again. Sniff the mixture. Which one is the stronger?

3 Repeat the double-spray test for all combinations of sprays. Is the strongest air freshener the same as the one you chose at the start as being the most powerful?

Experiment 70
Your favorite perfume

This experiment tests if people can identify different makes of manufactured perfumes.

1 You need a selection of perfumes, say three in all. You might be able to borrow them from an adult. Some special perfumes cost so much to buy that even one drop is very expensive!

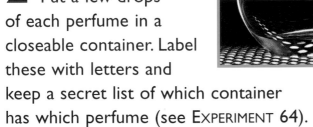

2 Put a few drops of each perfume in a closeable container. Label these with letters and keep a secret list of which container has which perfume (see EXPERIMENT 64).

3 Get friends to sniff each perfume in turn. Ask them to try to remember the scent in each one.

4 Next day, repeat step 3. But change the labels—only you know which perfume is in which container.

5 Do your friends now know which perfume is which? Did they guess that the containers have been changed or do they go by the labels on the containers?

Perfumes

Perfume is a pleasant-smelling mixture of alcohol and oil. It has been used for thousands of years.

Perfume is traditionally made by dissolving essential oils out of flowers using solvents and distilling the solution in a vacuum. One popular perfume—a strong scent called musk—was traditionally extracted from a gland of the male musk deer that lives in the forests of central Asia!

Although perfumes are still made from natural compounds, chemists have been able to identify their smell-producing ingredients, and many perfumes can now be made artificially.

Experiment 71
Make your own perfumes

Try mixing or blending your own perfume from common garden flowers. You might discover a new combination of scents that becomes a million dollar seller!

1 With permission from the gardener or owner, pick various flowers and herbs like roses, lavender, honeysuckles, azalea, and jasmine.

2 Follow the instructions for EXPERIMENT 62. With adult help, cut up, soak, and mash each flower in a little water. Filter the watery results into a set of separate containers.

3 Close or seal the containers. These are your stores or stocks of scent essences.

4 In a scientific way, blend a few drops of each essence with a few drops of one or two other essences. Try all the various combinations, and keep a record in your notebook.

5 Test each blend on your friends, as in EXPERIMENT 64. Which is most popular? Would you pay vast amounts of money for any of your homemade perfumes?

English scientist Robert Boyle (1627–1691) helped to establish the science of chemistry, and how to identify chemicals by their smell and other features. He devised some of the scientific laws about gases and air. His work is still used today by smell scientists.

Experiment 72
Smelly technology

The next two experiments use smell or scratch 'n' sniff cards or panels you find in toy stores, hobby stores, and joke equipment suppliers. Some of the smells are very strange!

There are also free samples of scents from perfumes and cosmetics in glossy magazines. The scent is released when you scratch a panel or lift a flap on the page.

1 You need a selection of smell or scratch 'n' sniff cards or panels, as described above. If you want to repeat the experiment and check the results, in true scientific fashion, collect several copies of each smell.

2 Place the smell cards on the table. Give each a key letter— A, B, and C. Make your own secret list that tells you about the smell in each card. But don't tell anyone else!

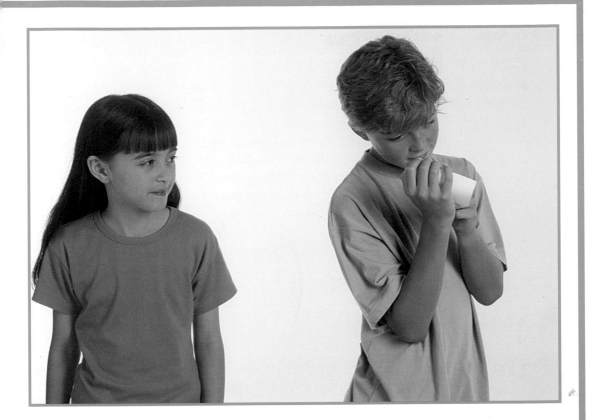

3 Write down the identities of the smells, as shown on your secret list, but without their key letters, and not in the right order. Let your friends see this list of smells.

4 Scratch one card and let your friends have a good sniff. Then they look at the list, and guess the smell. Record their answers in your notebook. Repeat for the other cards.

5 How many friends guessed correctly for each card? Did any of the friends change their minds about the identity of one of the early smells, when they sniffed a later one?

How do they work?

Scratch 'n' sniff technology is based on microscopic ball-shaped objects called encapsulated spherules. Each contains a tiny blob of the substance that has the smell—the odorant particles. The blob is contained or encapsulated in a thin "skin" of a plastic-like substance. When you scratch, rub, scrape, or tear it, the outer case breaks and releases the contents to float away in the air.

Smell detection

Each person or animal has his or her own individual smell. Each day we lose about 50 million skin cells, which fall to the ground, leaving a trail of our smell. Bloodhounds have been trained to pick up the scent of different people's trails, even if the people walk together. Dogs have a much more powerful sense of smell than we do because their smell membrane covers an area 35 times larger than ours.

Experiment 73
Smelling blind!

This experiment follows directly from EXPERIMENT 72, and is very similar. Except this time you do not show your friends a list of the smells. In fact, you give them no clues at all to the identities of the smells. Scientists call this "blind testing" because the tested people are "in the dark."

I You need a selection of smell or scratch 'n' sniff cards, a pen and paper, and some friends. Ask friends who were not involved in EXPERIMENT 72 as well as those who were. When you record the results, divide your friends into two groups according to whether they had participated in the previous experiment or not.

2 Place a set of smell cards on the table. Give each one a key letter—A, B, and C. Only you can see the secret list.

3 Give card A to your friends and ask them to have a good sniff. Ask them to guess what it is. Don't give any hints or clues. Don't agree or disagree. Try to remain neutral. Simply record their guesses in your notebook.

4 Give your friends a short break and then repeat step 3 for each of the other cards.

5 How many friends guessed correctly for each smell card? Compare the results with those from EXPERIMENT 72. The guesses for this experiment may not be so successful. People usually find it easier to choose from a list, rather than to guess completely "in the dark."

6 Now repeat the experiment yourself, but without leaving a break in between smelling. Select a smell card for a friend and ask them to select one for you. Cover up the identifying letter on the card and try to guess the identity of the smell card your partner has chosen. Immediately after try another card, and then a third. Make a note of the results. Is it more difficult to guess the identities of the smells when there is no break between smelling each card?

Smells all around
Smells—good and bad, pleasant, and nasty—are an important part of everyday life. Yet we rarely stop to think about them. These experiments will help you to understand the invisible world of scents and odors. Now you can be more aware of the smells, stinks, odors, and pongs around you, how you detect them, what they mean—and the effects they have on people's thoughts and moods. Happy sniffing!

Glossary of Terms

Absorption The process of being soaked up or of soaking up something.

Acetone A colorless liquid that mixes with water and is flammable (will catch fire easily). It is used to produce certain chemicals and as a thinner for paints.

Acrylic An artificial fiber that is made from acrylic acid.

Adhesion The ability of one substance to stick to another.

Alkaloids A group of compounds containing nitrogen which are found in plants. They react with proteins and change their structure.

Anaesthetic This is a drug which causes a loss of sensation applied to a patient before an operation to stop them feeling pain.

Antennae A pair of "feelers" (like two thick hairs) attached to the heads of insects which enable them to feel, smell, and taste.

Aroma A subtle and usually pleasant smell, often produced by spices and plants.

Aromatherapy The practice of applying aromatic oils and creams (made from plant extracts) to the skin and massaging them to produce relaxation and cure complaints.

Aromatic essence The essential part of an aromatic substance, usually an oil.

Atoms The smallest parts of all elements. Each atom has a nucleus at its center, which contains protons and neutrons and then has electrons spinning around the outside.

Cepiates The smell particles given off when the flesh of an onion is cut.

Chlorine A greenish toxic gas. A diluted form is often used as an ingredient in disinfectants.

Circuit A pathway for electricity to flow around.

Circuit board The base upon which a circuit is mounted. It is usually made from a special insulating material.

Cohesion The ability of the particles in a substance to stick together. Substances with high cohesion stretch rather than break up when they are pulled. Substances with low cohesion separate when they are pulled.

Compound This is a combination of two or more elements joined together.

Concave (diverging) lens This lens bends light beams so that they spread apart, making things look smaller (diminished). Concave lenses are dish-shaped and thinner in the middle than at the edge.

Conductor Any substance which allows electricity to flow freely through it.

Conjunctivas The delicate covers which protect the eyeballs and eyelids.

Consistency The degree to which a substance is thick or thin, runny or firm.

Convex (converging) lens This lens bends light beams so that they come together, making things look bigger (magnified). Convex lenses bulge and are thicker in the middle than around the edge.

Critical angle The angle where refraction becomes reflection, when light rays hit a surface at a shallow angle.

Denaturing To change the nature or make up of something.

Density The thickness or heaviness of a substance according to the mass of its particles and how they are packed. Substances with a high density have tightly packed heavy particles and those with low density have loosely packed light particles.

Discharge The loss of electric charge.

Dissolves To make something go into solution e.g. water dissolves sugar.

Distilling To purify by boiling a liquid (to get a gas) and then condensing (turn back to a liquid or solid) the vapor by cooling.

Dropper An instrument with a flexible bulb on the end of a glass or plastic tube. Small "drops" of liquid can be drawn up and released by squeezing the bulb.

Edible When something is suitable for human consumption (eating).

Electrical conduction The transmission of electricity.

Electric current The quantity of electricity flowing around a circuit, measured in "amps."

Electricity Electricity is a form of energy in the form of charged particles, such as stationary or moving electrons and ions.

Electromagnet A magnet created by

winding a coil of wire around iron or steel through which a current can then be passed.

Electromagnetic spectrum The whole range of electromagnetic rays and waves, from light rays to gamma rays, X-rays, ultraviolet rays, and also radio and TV rays.

Electrostatic A stationary electrical charge often produced by rubbing certain insulators together.

Electrostatic attraction When an electrostatically charged object pulls or attracts another object.

Extract To take something away from something else, to draw it out.

Fiber-optic filament A tiny strand, made of glass or plastic, through which light can pass.(Used in fiber-optic instruments.)

Filter paper "Porous" paper that allows liquid to pass through but not solids.

Focal length The distance from the center of the lens to the focal point.

Focal point (focus) The point at which converging light rays meet.

Funnel A utensil used for pouring liquids with a wide mouth joined to a narrow tube.

Habituation Apparently fading with time—i.e. a smell starts off strong and gradually seems to get weaker.

Horizontal The term used to describe something level and flat that is parallel to where the Earth meets the sky, i.e. the horizon.

Hydrogen sulfide The gas that has a smell of rotten eggs.

Incident beam The incoming ray of light.

Insulator Any material which does not allow electricity to pass through it, also known as non-conducting.

Internal reflection When light is reflected within a substance.

Jupiter The largest planet in the solar system, fifth from the Sun.

Lens Curved shape of transparent substance, such as glass or plastic.

Light spectrum The range of colors in white light.

Light switch A device used for opening or closing the electric circuit for an electric light, to turn it on or off.

Lunar eclipse This occurs when the Earth passes between the Sun and the Moon, and the Earth casts its shadow on the Moon.

Magnetic field An invisible magnetic force which affects a certain area of space.

Magnetism An invisible force which attracts certain materials towards each other. In the context of electricity, it is the force that acts between electric currents.

Magnify To make something appear larger than its actual size.

Meteorites Solid pieces of a rock or metal that fall to Earth from space because they are too big to be burned up by the Earth's atmosphere.

Methane gas This is a colorless, odorless gas that forms the main part of natural gas.

Microscope An instrument that uses different-sized lenses to make objects look bigger at a close distance.

Mineral A non-living chemical compound (not from a plant or an animal) occurring naturally on the Earth.

Molecule This is the smallest and simplest single particle of a compound.

Mucus A sticky substance produced by a body's mucus membranes.

Muslin A thin cotton fabric.

Nasal cavity The hollow chamber just behind your nose.

Negative When something is negatively charged—shown with a minus (–) sign.

Neon This is a rare colorless gas.

Neon light A bright light produced when a glass tube is filled with gas, and electric current is passed through it.

Nerve signals Messages sent by the nerves to and from the brain.

Neutralizer A substance that can cancel out the effect of another substance.

Nitrous oxide A slightly soluble sweet smelling gas once used as an anaesthetic, also known as "laughing gas."

Nucleus This is the positively charged (+) region at the center of an atom made up of protons and neutrons (plural **nuclei**).

Odor / Odorants The part of a substance that gives it a characteristic smell.

Olfactory patches Two patches of nerve cells in the roof of the nasal cavity which are sensitive to smells in the air and enable us to smell things.

Opaque When light cannot pass through something, it is said to be opaque.

Optical fibers Tiny rods made of special glass through which light can travel for long distances. (See fiber optic filament.)

Optics The science related to the behavior of light and how this affects vision.

Ostwald viscometer A type of viscometer, named after Friedrich Ostwald, which measures the time taken for a liquid to run down a very thin capillary tube.

Palate The shelf which forms the roof of the mouth and base of the nasal cavity.

"Parallel" Batteries connected in a circuit side by side, parallel to each other.

Particle A very small piece of something.

Periscope An optical instrument which allows you to see something not in your direct line of vision: from inside a submarine to see above the surface of the water.

Permanent magnet A magnet which always has magnetic properties.

Pestle (and mortar) A pestle is a club-shaped instrument for grinding material and a mortar is a bowl-shaped container in which the material is ground.

Photons The tiny energetic particles that make up light.

Polarized light Where some light waves are filtered out, so those that remain ripple in one direction rather than in many directions.

Polarizing filters Filters which cut out certain light waves.

Pollution Damage to the environment by harmful substances, such as "acid rain" (rain containing sulfur dioxide released by burning coal or oil) which harms life forms.

Positive When something is positively charged. This is shown with a plus (+) sign.

Potential difference (voltage) The pushing strength of electricity around a circuit.

Potpourri Dried flower petals often used as a room fragrance.

Pourability The ability of a substance to be poured from one container into another.

Preserving This means preventing something from decaying or changing.

Prism A solid flat-sided object made of glass or plastic. Prisms are used to bend light in optical instruments and to split light into colors.

Proteins A group of compounds found in all living organisms. They are most commonly found in certain foods, such as meat and fish, which the body needs for healthy development and growth.

Pulp The state of a material which has been mashed e.g. mashed potato.

Rayon (viscose fiber) A synthetic fiber made from the cellulose in wood pulp. (Cellulose makes up the main part of a plant cell wall.)

Reflection When light bounces off an object.

Refraction The bending of light as it passes from one transparent substance to another.

Refractive index The comparison of the angles of incidence and refraction. The higher the refractive index, the more the light bends.

Repel To force something away: a positively charged object repels another positively charged object. (The opposite of attract.)

Resistance How much a circuit resists, or prevents, electricity from flowing. Resistance is measured in "ohms."

Resistors Materials which resist the passage of electricity but do not stop it completely.

Saliva A substance produced by the mouth that softens food to help us to swallow. Saliva also contains enzymes, which help to break down and dissolve food in the process of digestion.

Sap A solution made up of mineral salts and sugars that forms the life fluid circulating inside plants.

"Series" Batteries connected in a circuit end to end, one after another.

Shadow A dark shape cast on a surface when light rays strike an opaque body.

Slit-beam A thin beam of almost parallel light rays filtered through a thin slit.

Smell membrane A thin layer of skin, inside the nose, containing the olfactory patches.

Solar eclipse When the Moon passes between the Sun and the Earth, the Moon casts its shadow on the Earth.

Solvent A liquid which dissolves another substance.

Soy sauce A salty dark brown sauce made from soybeans, and used mainly in Far Eastern cooking.

Static electricity An electric charge produced by friction such as rubbing two insulators together.

Telescope An instrument which uses lenses to make things in the distance look nearer.

Terminal The place where the electrical current enters or leaves the circuit.

Texture The surface of a substance usually detected by the senses of touch and taste.

Translucent When something allows light to partially pass through it—although light passes through it, the view will be blurred.

Transparent When you can see clearly through something, it is said to be transparent.

Unpolarized light Waves of light rippling in all directions—daylight is an example.

Vacuum Empty space containing no matter.

Variable resistors Device used to cause a variation in the strength of electricity passed through something such as the volume control knob on a radio or the dimmer on a light switch.

Virtual focal point The imaginary place in front of the lens from which light rays "appear" to originate.

Viscometer A piece of apparatus used in science laboratories to measure viscosity.

Viscosity The measure of a substance's resistance to flow. Substances with "high viscosity" do not flow very easily (such as syrup), whereas substances with "low viscosity" flow very easily (such as water or milk).

Viscous Thick and sticky, usually used to describe the state of a slow-flowing liquid.

Volts The unit of measurement for the pushing strength of electricity around a circuit.

Index

A
absorption, 56–7
adhesion, 44–5
adhesion, 47
air fresheners, 84–5
Alhazen, 14
alkaloids, 61
amber, 28, 60
anesthetic, 82
Apollo 12 spacecraft, 11
armchair science, 54, 55
aromatherapy, 83
essences, aromatic , 76
atoms, 24
attraction, adhesive, 45
attraction, electrostatic, 26–7, 28

B
batteries, electric, 30, 31
batteries, connected in parallel, 32
connected in series, 32
beam, incident, 13
beam, reflected, 13
bloodhounds, 90
board, insulating, 33
Boyle, Robert, 88

breathing system, human, 82
bubbles, 21

C
capillary tube, 51
cepiates, 77
charge, negative, 24, 29
charge, positive, 29
charge, separating, 24
chlorine gas, 75
circuit, electrical, 30, 31, 36
cohesion in slimes, 46, 47
color, 21, 22
coloring of slimes, 58
concave, 15, 18, 20
conductor, electrical, 28, 30, 33, 34
conjunctivas, 77
consistency, 42
converge, 18
convex, 15, 18, 19
critical angle, 17
Cross, Charles, 61
current, electric, 30, 36

D
Davy, Humphry, 82

denaturing, 61
diverge, 18
dust on TV screens, 27

E
Earth, 11, 20
eclipse, solar, 11
eggs, 61, 81
Egyptians, Ancient, 76
electricity, 23–37
electricity, dangers of, 23
electricity, static, 24–5, 26–7, 28, 29, 35
electromagnet, 35, 36, 37
electromagnetic spectrum, 55
electrons in atom, 24
energy source, 5
extracting smells, 76

F
Faraday, Michael, 37
fibers, artificial, 61
filtering slimes, 57
flashlight, danger of, 5
fluid dynamics, 41
fluids, 43
focal length, 19, 20

focal point, 19, 20
   virtual, 20
focus, 19
friction, 24
fruit, sliminess of, 60

G
Galileo Galilei, 20
gelatins, viscosity of, 55
glass, frosted, 6
glues, 44–5, 60

H
habituation, 75
hair, flyaway, 25
Henry, Joseph, 37
"Hungary Water," 76
hydrogen sulfide gas,
   80, 81

I
insulator, electrical, 33, 34

J
Jupiter, 20

K
Kepler, Johannes, 9

L
"laughing gas," 82
Lavoisier, Antoine, 80
lens, 18–20
light, 5–22
   bulbs, 5, 6, 12, 23
   rays, 8, 11, 15, 16, 17,
    20
   sources, 12
   waves, 21, 22

M
magnetic field, 35–6
magnetism, 35–7
magnifier, 18
Maxwell, James Clerk, 55
membrane, dog's smell, 90
microbes, 20
microscope, 20
mirror-images, 14
mirrors, 12, 14
   curving, 15
molecule, 45
molecules, 46
Moon, 11, 20
moth, emperor, 73

mucus, animal, 63
   human, 40, 82
mud, 62
musk, 86

N
nasal cavity, 70–1
neon lights, 37
nitrous oxide gas, 82
nose, human, 65, 75
nucleus, of atom, 24

O
oils, essential, 83, 86
onions, 77
opaque, 6–7, 11, 17
optics, 5
orbits, planetary, 9
Ostwald, Freidrich, 51, 59

P
palate, human, 70–1
particles, odorant, 66, 70,
   72, 75, 77, 89
pascal (scientific unit), 43
Pascal's Law, 43
Pascal, Blaise, 43
patches, olfactory, 66
perfumes, 85, 86
   make your own, 86–7
periscope, 15
planetary motion, laws
   of, 9
Poiseulle, Jean, 59
pourability, 53
pressure, effect on viscosity
   of, 43
prism, 22
proteins, 61
pythons, 63

R
rainbow, 21, 22
rayon, manufacturing
   process of, 61
reflection, 12, 13, 14, 17,
   21
refraction, 16, 17, 19, 21
refractive index, 16
resin, 60
reverse shadow, 9

S
saliva, human, 40
sap, sliminess of plant, 60

Scheele, Carl Wilhelm, 75
scratch 'n' sniff cards, 88–9
senses, five human, 66
senses, test of, 67, 68–9, 70
shadows, 6, 8, 9, 10–11
shark's sense of smell, 69
sight, sense of, 5
slimes, 38–64
   in nature, 40, 62–3, 64
   dangers of, 39, 62
slimometer, 50–1, 52
slit-beam, 13, 19, 21
smell of individual person,
   90
smells, 65–91
smells popularity table,
   78–9
smells, recalling memories,
   82
smells, strength of, 72–3,
   74–5
snakes, not slimy, 63
Snel, Willebrord, 16
solvents, 56
spectrum, light, 22
spherules, encapsulated, 89
Stoke's Law, 41
Stokes, George, 41
submarines, 15
sulfur, 80
Sun, 5, 11, 12, 20
switch, electrical, 30

T
telescope, 20
temperature, effect on slimes
   of, 48–9
terminal, battery, 30
Thales of Greece, 28
translucent, 6–7, 8
transparent, 6–7

V
van Leeuwenhoek, Anton,
   20
viscometers, 51, 59
viscosity, 41, 42–3, 47, 49,
   55
Volta, Alessandro, 31
voltage, 32

W
water, 28
wire, insulated, 36, 37
wiring, electrical, 23